COMMITMENT

COMMITMENT

Portraits by Morton I. Hamburg

Text by Kashmir Hill

Cider Mill Press Book Publishers
Kennebunkport, Maine

COMMITMENT

13-Digit ISBN: 978-1-60433-334-3
10-Digit ISBN: 1-60433-334-0

Cider Mill Press Book Publishers
"Where good books are ready for press"
12 Port Farm Road
Kennebunkport, Maine 04046

Visit us on the Web!
www.cidermillpress.com

This book may be ordered by mail from the publisher. Please include $6.95 for postage and handling. Please support your local bookseller first!

Books published by Cider Mill Press Book Publishers are available at special discounts for bulk purchases in the United States by corporations, institutions, and other organizations. For more information, please contact the publisher.

Front cover design by Whitney Cookman
Interior design by Pamela Geismar
Photograph of Catherine "Cat" and Jennifer Cora, 2012, by David Carlson, Los Angeles

Printed in the United States of America

2 3 4 5 6 7 8 9 0

First Edition

TO MY BROTHER, Dr. Marvin Hamburg. He has always been the personification of commitment—in the absence of our hard-working parents, he was committed to taking care of me as a child in Brooklyn, although only seven years older than me; he was committed at 20 to fighting for his country against the Nazis at the Bridge of Remagen, Germany, earning a Bronze Star and a Purple Heart. He has always been devoted to his wife, children and grandchildren; was a superb camp counselor to the freshmen group at Camp Mooween; committed to practicing good dentistry, as well as teaching many American and foreign students at the NYU Dental School; committed to being a caring friend and neighbor to many in New York and in Florida; using his charm and wisdom to carry out his great genealogical studies; and most of all, for being committed throughout his 88 years to life itself.

I also dedicate my work to my beautiful grandchild, Stella Louise Kirk Hamburg, who I know will be as committed to her work (whatever she chooses to do) as her wonderful parents, John L. Hamburg and Christina Kirk, and her Aunt Elizabeth, are to theirs.

— M. I. Hamburg

TO MY GREAT-GRANDMOTHER, Anita Hurless, whose fitful memory in her later years caused her to ask me daily—and sometimes multiple times daily—what I wanted to do when I grew up. Telling a woman I loved so fiercely that I wanted to be a writer over and over again may have ensured that I pursued a path that seemed impractical and fanciful when I grew older. She helped me commit mentally at an early age to a career that I now love.

— Kashmir Hill

Contents

Acknowledgments

THE CREATION OF THIS WORK, as with any book, depended upon the contributions of many people. This has been a collaborative effort. We appreciate the work of those who introduced us to the publisher, as well as those who helped us arrange for the couples to be photographed and interviewed.

We, naturally, thank each of the couples who contributed their time, energy and honesty to making this book so unique. It is not just a photography book; it is about relationships. We are very much indebted to those whose relationships are reviewed here. Hopefully, their efforts will prove very meaningful to those who contemplate being a part of such a relationship.

In addition, each of us would like to offer the following personal thanks.

Morton I. Hamburg:

I am grateful to, and acknowledge the extraordinary talents and dedication of, Pamela Geismar, for so ably carrying out the design of this book and its cover.

I am also grateful to Gabe Greenberg, one of the best photo-editors in the country. He really knows how to take a simple photograph of people and make them look beautiful and handsome. Thanks also to Lear Levin for bringing me to Gabe, and for his thoughts about photography.

I would never have been able to bring this follow-up project to fruition but for my wife, Joan Hamburg, and my fantastic children, Elizabeth and John, who again supported me at every turn. Thanks also to my daughter-in-law, Christina Kirk, and my almost-son-in-law, Roberto De Mitri, for saying and doing nice things.

Acknowledgments

Kashmir Hill:

I am thankful to my journalism school professor, David Margolick, who was a wonderful mentor in graduate school and kind enough to introduce me to Mort Hamburg when he sought a writing partner for this book. I appreciate Mort Hamburg's trusting me with this project though I was single (and thus, uncommitted) when we first started it. Due to my conversations with him and with the wonderful couples in these pages, I have come to better appreciate one of life's greatest pleasures.

Children first come to understand the nature of commitment through their parents' devotion. I want to thank my parents, Thomas and Dottie Hill and Monica Oriti, for their unconditional support and for encouraging me to pursue what I love, throughout my life. And I'm also grateful to my sisters, Radiance Chapman and Scheherazade Hill, for giving me strength whenever mine wanes.

Photographer's Note

IN 2000, having given up the practice of law after almost 50 years, I embarked on a new career with the encouragement of my wife and children. I decided to become a full-time photographer and to produce a book about couples, all of whom were married and very much committed to each other. It was called *Couples: The Meaning of Commitment*. I photographed 35 couples, and text was written by a terrific writer, Catherine Whitney. The book was published by Andrews McMeel, and sold over 16,000 hardcover copies. It is still selling on Amazon.com.

Over the years, I received a number of comments about the book, most quite favorable. However, a number of people asked why I included only heterosexual married couples, and not men and women who had lived together for a long time, were very committed to each other, but chose never to marry, as well as same-sex couples.

So a few years ago, I started on a new book of photographs of and text about all sorts of couples. Catherine Whitney was unavailable to be my collaborator and, fortunately, our mutual friend, David Margolick, recommended his former journalism student Kashmir Hill to me as my writer-collaborator. Kashmir has done a brilliant job of interviewing and writing about each of the couples in this book. She asked each couple what they thought was the meaning of commitment; why they had gotten together and/or married; and why they had stayed together.

As before, I decided to use the natural setting of the couples' homes or workplaces. In one case, while Judy Collins was appearing again at the Café Carlyle in New York, I was able to photograph Judy and her husband, Louis Nelson, at the apartment given to them by the Carlyle while Judy sang there. I essentially used only a Nikon 700 digital camera, and sometimes a flash. The very talented photo-editor Gabe Greenberg converted the color images to black and white for this book, and everyone looks great.

There is no special way to convey love and commitment through a photograph, but I have tried. I hope that this will not only encourage many people to evidence their commitment to others but also to recognize that commitment to anything or anyone is the secret to success in everything.

—Morton I. Hamburg

Introduction

Peter Drucker
Management: Tasks, Responsibilities, Practices

MANY LOVE STORIES are full of promise and hope: two young people falling madly in love and pledging their lives to one another. That is where most of the stories spun in books and films end.

"And they lived happily ever after…" is the way fairy tales and Disney movies conclude their tales of adventurous characters who fend off villains while tumbling into love. Children grow up fixated on finding the heart's one true love and not on the long and complicated story so quickly dismissed with that short phrase "ever after." There's no sense of what it's like to grow old with Prince Charming or to raise children with Cinderella.

The 2009 Disney/Pixar film *Up* was a delightful departure from that mode of relationship storytelling. The film starts with a flight-obsessed little boy meeting a little girl who also sports an aviator's cap. The story of their courtship, marrying and growing old together is told montage-style within the first 10 minutes of the movie, with beautiful moments—picnics, house-painting, and holding hands—mixed with poignant moments of heartache—a car tire gone flat, a baby lost, and a dream trip they're never able to afford. His wife's death in old age leads the then-78-year-old man to embark on a house-floating adventure to fulfill a promise he had made to her when they first met as kids. It was the rare tale for children about the complicated long-term nature of commitment rather than the simple and straightforward joys of initial infatuation.

Peter Drucker's famous quote about commitment comes not from a romance but from a book on management, specifically a chapter on business performance. It seemed appropriate, for commitment in love and in work are not so unalike. In both, there is a belief and faith that giving yourself to the project will yield greater returns. While love provides the fodder for dreams and fantasies, commitment is the foundation for building a future.

The nature of commitment is what is explored here in photos and in text. This book is a sequel to *Couples: A Celebration of Commitment*, which, a decade ago, told the tales of couples who had discovered the secrets of marriage and relationship longevity. This book seeks to expand on that initial foray into love and devotion—exploring the "why" rather than the "how" of commitment. Like the first, this book includes a number of married men and women. But this time, there are also persons who have been together for decades without marrying, and same-sex couples, such as Iron Chef "Cat" Cora and her partner, Jennifer, for whom the nature of commitment has become a politically charged matter as the country engages in state-by-state debates over who has the right to marry.

The book does not seek to impart the secrets of a successful relationship, or how you know when you've met "the one," or how to make a relationship last—though it may brush up against those things. Instead, it is about finding the meaning of the word, *commitment*. I'll start with a few things that commitment is not.

IT IS NOT SCARY

Not every couple in this book was comfortable with the word. "Commitment has so many negative connotations," joked Susie Essman, who plays an irascible on-screen wife on HBO's *Curb Your Enthusiasm*. "Like, you're going to be 'committed' to an insane asylum. Or you're going to 'commit' a crime."

It can be an intimidating word, even when not associated with mental health issues and illegal activities. It is a word laden with the weight of obligations and responsibility. However, it is lightened when paired with that which is gained from it: a task completed, a debt repaid, a goal reached. It is even more satisfying when the commitment is reciprocal—made to and shared with another person.

In the same interview, Essman described her commitment to husband, Jim Harder, as "safety," saying that what "we all want in our lives is to feel protected and loved and safe."

Even in the romantic context, though, people often talk about being "scared of commitment." Catherine Whitney, the wonderful writer of the first *Couples* book, captured the imprecision of that expression well. "No one really fears commitment," she wrote. "We fear breaking apart, not coming together."

There are some, though, who do see the bonds of coming together as restrictive—who chafe at the idea of trading in selfishness for safety. Television executive Ed Bleier was a bachelor in his 40s when he met his wife, Magda, a young French journalist working in Philadelphia. Having been single for so long, Ed was quite anxious about the idea of getting married. When Magda told him, though, that she was going to leave the country if he wasn't serious about their relationship, his anxiety took a new form.

"Suddenly I was more worried about losing her than gaining her," Ed said.

IT IS NOT A PIECE OF PAPER

A marriage ceremony is an outward sign of commitment, but is not commitment itself—especially these days when divorces are so easily, and frequently, obtained. "A piece of paper does not a commitment make," says Joy Behar, who has been with her partner, now husband, Steve Janowitz since the 1980s. They only moved in together after September 11, 2001; in a time when the world suddenly seemed so fragile, their commitment was comfortingly concrete.

Bryan Batt, a long-time actor known to many as the ad designer on TV's *Mad Men*, is frustrated over his home state of Louisiana not granting him and his partner Tom Cianfinchi the right to wed, but says that makes their relationship even deeper on some level. "What I love about our commitment is that we wake up and there is no piece of paper. We don't have a legal binding ceremony or document that keeps us together," Bryan said. "Every morning, we wake up and make that decision to be together. And we've been making that decision every day for the last 22 years."

Bryan, said though, that if marriage were an option in Louisiana, he and Tom would choose it. Part of the pleasure of commitment is declaring it publicly and letting family and friends partake in the declaration in a formal ceremony. The markers—the wedding march, vows, and rings—are as much for others as for the couple.

The dulcet-voiced Judy Collins and her husband, Louis Nelson, a talented industrial designer, were happily together for 18 years before getting married. But they wanted the ritual of the actual wedding ceremony.

"It resonates. It's ancient. For us, at our age, marriage wasn't about having children," says Collins, who was in her 50s when she married Nelson. "It was about emotional commitment. Something shifted—a strong, powerful, unseen force—that indicated this was a safe place to be emotionally. And there's a different tranquility when you have that kind of emotional security. I felt that security in our relationship, but the wedding sealed it."

It's a tranquility that all couples should be entitled to.

Architect Evan Galen and advertising executive Steve Novick did get married during the brief period in 2008 when same-sex marriage was legalized in California, which they wanted in order to legally be able to take care of each other. They had been together for decades by that point, their commitment firmly established. The marriage license bore no symbolic meaning for them—it is simply a necessity so that the state will recognize the role they play in one other's lives should one of them be in the hospital. The commitment is only marked by their marriage license, not made by it.

"Commitment is as much unspoken and unwritten, as it is anything else," says Steve. "It's an inherent, ongoing quality of your life. It's not something you have to affirm with a certificate."

Still, denying certain couples the right to affirm their commitment with a certificate is an ugly thing. Jennifer and Catherine "Cat" Cora have four children together but had to hire a lawyer for an adoption process for the children they had each conceived and carried. Frustrated, they predict the country will one day look back on this time as we now look back on segregation and discrimination before the Civil Rights Act. Commitment is already equal opportunity; one day, marriage likely will be too.

IT IS NOT STATIC

Describing commitment as "safety" makes one think of a net that is always there to catch you. Indeed, a springy, elastic safety net may be the best way in which to conceive it. Every couple balked at describing commitment as something hard and fast. World-renowned artists April Gornik and Eric Fischl emphasized the evolution that has taken place, and continues to occur, in their relationship.

"People change and grow," April said. "Commitment has to be fluid and in motion and active."

Many described their commitment as "day by day"—waking up every morning and making the decision to recommit. It's a mix of being able to take your partner's love and support for granted, and assessing the relationship regularly to ensure that you are making each other happy enough to justify its continuance.

"That's what always terrified me about marriage: the idea of settling down, of becoming one unit, and then becoming something static and unchanging," said Kathryn Grody, a wonderful actress married to the brilliant performer Mandy Patinkin.

"In fact, you keep evolving who you are. After 30 years, I think commitment is re-choosing on a continual basis to re-embrace aspects of this person," says Kathryn.

IT MAKES YOU A BETTER PERSON

The couples we chose for this book are an accomplished group, excelling in finance, media, medicine, law, entertainment, and the arts. Many of them say that their commitment to their partner or spouse at home helped lay the groundwork for their professional success.

"You don't take for granted the love and support, but you do in a way," said private equity banker David Shapiro, who is married to writer Abigail Pogrebin. "You know it will be there and it makes you stronger. It allows me to go out and live my life outside my family the way I do. I can stride confidently through my day knowing that I have that base at home."

It's not just about having stability in their personal lives. Many of the couples talked about the ways a partner encouraged him or her to be a better person. A shared commitment to self-improvement is a recurring theme throughout the book.

"For me, commitment has been Bruce pushing me to be the very best that I can be, and giving me the opportunity and space to excel as a person," said art dealer Barbara Berger.

"Commitment is ensuring that the other person is as happy as you are, and that each of you is maximizing your goals in life," said her husband, Bruce.

We usually think of commitment as a kind of sacrifice—a giving of the self to another.

Ed Bleier related it back to Austrian philosopher Martin Buber's concept of how humans actualize their existence: "The feelings of self are so profoundly improved by the ability to have a commitment to someone else that you not only love the somebody else but you like yourself even more because you're able to give the love."

Perhaps we like ourselves even more for another reason. An article in the *New York Times* at the beginning of 2011 reported on research into what makes for the happiest and most sustainable marriages. In any relationship, we expand ourselves through our partner's knowledge and experiences. According to the *Times*, "research shows that the more self-expansion people experience from their partner, the more committed and satisfied they are in the relationship." One researcher coined the term the "Michelangelo effect" to describe the way partners sculpt one another to help each other achieve their goals.

The "Michelangelo effect" reveals a self-serving side of commitment. Ideally, we choose to commit ourselves to partners most likely to mold us into better people.

COMMITMENT'S MANY MEANINGS

When asked for her meaning of commitment, one interviewee asked if I'd looked it up in the dictionary. *The American Heritage Dictionary* offers up 12 meanings. The most important one for our purposes is "a pledge or promise; obligation."

Comedienne Anne Meara tapped into that definition when describing the meaning of commitment in the context of her six decades of marriage to actor Jerry Stiller. She put it very simply: "You try to keep your promise. That's all."

Some people were brief in their definitions of commitment and others were effusive. We encountered a multitude of meanings given by the couples interviewed. The meaning of the word would seem to be as fluid and expansive as is commitment itself. Some words came up over and over again: "trust," "loyalty," "respect," "love." And also "luck." There is a certain leap of faith in tying one's life to that of another, and trusting that their desire to be bound will remain constant. Many people thanked Lady Luck for helping them to find that right person.

To most, commitment means safety and support. It seemingly means loyalty and trust. It usually means being bound, but also being freed from the fear of being alone. It often means having your partner's needs, goals, dreams, sorrows and joys become your own. It probably means encouraging one another to be better people. It hopefully means that love has taken root and flowered season after season.

Commitment would seem to be the "ever after," in which two people are brought closer together by sharing happy times and by helping each other through difficult ones. Without commitment, our lives' stories are far less rich and satisfying.

— *Kashmir Hill*

COMMITMENT

Joy Behar & Steve Janowitz
Love of the Heart, Mind, and Funny Bone

IN THE BEGINNING of Joy Behar's stand-up comedienne career in the 1980s, the recently divorced English schoolteacher used to joke that she "wanted a man in her life, but not in her apartment." The co-host of *The View* was true to her joke for many years.

She and Steve met in 1982 at a singles weekend in Woodstock, New York. "It was basically for single hippies," says Joy. "No children were allowed, and there was semi-nudity. Some people were naked, and some were not. We were not."

Both had been invited by friends to attend. "I went up there to meet a man," continues Joy.

"I just went up there to get away for the weekend," Steve replies. "I had no expectation for a big relationship."

Both native New Yorkers—as evident in their accents—and schoolteachers—formerly in Joy's case, and Steve now retired—they had much in common, including a wicked sense of humor. They met during a screening of Roman Polanski's *Knife in the Water*. "If we'd known [Polanski] was a pedophile at the time, we wouldn't have watched it," says Joy. "But we still would have gone on a date."

The stages of commitment have come more slowly to these two than to most couples. They dated for almost two decades before they finally moved in together, Steve moving from the Bronx into Joy's apartment in the Upper West Side of Manhattan. (Eve, Joy's daughter from her prior marriage, lives in the same building.)

Why did they finally move in together after dating for almost 20 years? A nation's loss made them want to be closer to one another.

"It was right after 9/11," says Joy. "A lot of people got married after that. A lot of people got pregnant, but that was not in the cards for us. So we moved in."

Though their living arrangements changed, the fundamentals of their relationship didn't. They say the only difference after moving in together was "less wearing out of the tread on Steve's tires."

In 2009, Joy mentioned to Barbara Walters on air that she and Steve had talked about marriage for practical reasons; Walters immediately offered to host the wedding at her house. The aside led to a flurry of media headlines, including an article in *People* magazine.

Three months later, Joy and Steve changed their minds. The tabloid media reported that it was because Joy was sick of people talking about it. But Joy says that wasn't the real reason. "I got busy," she says. In June 2009, she announced that she would start hosting her own show, *The Joy Behar Show*, on HLN, in addition to appearing on *The View*.

"A piece of paper does not a commitment make. We have a commitment based on love and respect," says Joy. "And not having anywhere else to go," she adds, laughing.

Joy and Steve describe their commitment as something that has evolved extremely naturally, without much pushing by either one of them. "We've been committed since the beginning without even realizing it," says Steve. "Over time, it just became an understanding that we always looked out for each other. I always cared about Joy more than anyone else. And as you would for anyone that you love, the other person's welfare is going to be more important than yours sometimes."

Joy still keeps a busy television schedule, while Steve is now retired. They like how their relationship has evolved so naturally over the years.

"When you're committed, you know it; you don't have to think about it, you can feel it," says Steve. "You don't have to get down on one knee and decide, 'Now, I'm committed.'"

Joy adds: "First of all, you can't get down on one knee at our age. You might not be able to get up!" ※

A few months after this interview, in August 2011, Joy and Steve were married at a small ceremony in Manhattan, where the book's photographer, Mort Hamburg, serenaded them with "More I Cannot Wish You." They are still committed.

Susie Essman & Jim Harder | Uncurbed Affection

SUSIE ESSMAN HAD TWO HUSBANDS at her wedding in September 2008: the love of her life, Jim Harder, and her small-screen hubby, Jeff Garlin, who plays Jeff Greene on HBO's *Curb Your Enthusiasm.*

The wedding was a small one, for immediate family only. Susie and Jim didn't feel the need to make a big deal of it at their ages—she, 53, and he, 51. But Garlin called the night before to say he was in town and wound up crashing the wedding.

"It seemed appropriate to have both of my husbands at the wedding, actually," says Susie, who's far less foul-mouthed and irascible than the character she plays on HBO's longest-running series. "I've been married to Jeff longer than Jim. That relationship is funnier, but horrible. He's always cheating on me!"

Susie's real-life marriage is a much healthier, loving, and affectionate one. When in the same room, she and Jim are almost always touching each other in some way, still like newlyweds after two years of marriage and seven years of being together.

"We very easily could not have met," says Susie. She had been friends with Jim's older brother, Mike, for years, but he never thought to introduce them. A mutual friend, who was a casting director, told her, though, that Mike's brother was "hot." When Susie heard that Jim was going to be in Manhattan for Thanksgiving in 2003, she called Mike and said she needed help shopping for martini glasses. He said that his brother would have to tag along—Susie did not mind.

She and Jim, a real estate developer, hit it off right away. "Casting and matchmaking must go hand in hand," says Jim. But Jim lived in upstate New York, was launching a second career, and had four children in their teens and tweens from his first marriage.

"The first thing he told me was that he didn't want to get involved," says Susie. "I said, 'Who said I want to get involved?' But then all of a sudden, we were involved."

"The cards worked out," says Jim. "The timing was not necessarily perfect, but it turned out to be perfect. You can never tell if the timing is right or not."

They started dating slowly—seeing each other every other weekend. Susie didn't want to jump into the lives of his children, then aged 10 to 15, unless they were sure they were going to be together for the long term. By 2006, they were sure and bought a house near Albany.

"I committed to an entire family," says Susie. "I committed not just to him but to four teenagers."

And she loves it. Being a mother to the children through their teenage years has been a tremendous joy for her. "It's been great. What else are you supposed to do with your life?" she asks.

They entered their relationship and marriage knowing that they wanted to share their lives. "Commitment is covering each other's back, being patient, working to understand each other," says Jim. In his wedding vows, Jim promised to "protect Susie from all the villains."

"That really struck me," says Susie. "That there's somebody there who's going to protect me no matter what. Commitment is safety. I think what we all want in our lives is to feel protected and loved and safe."

Lest there be too much sincerity in one sitting from this comedienne, she jokes about the word *commitment*, a topic she also riffs on in her book, *What Would Susie Say?: Bullsh*t Wisdom About Love, Life and Comedy*.

"The word has so many negative connotations. Like, you're going to be committed to an insane asylum. You're going to commit a crime," she says, explaining why it may have taken her so many years to commit herself.

"In a good relationship, commitment is easy. You don't really think about it. You're just in it," Susie continues. "But the commitment part comes from doing the things you love on the days you don't necessarily feel like doing them. And that's commitment in all things—your work, your kids, your spouse."

Jim adds curiosity as an important element of their relationship. "We're always wanting to know more about each other," says Jim. "Life doesn't stay the same."

"It's fluid. And you have to recommit all the time," adds Susie. They have moments when they consciously recommit, knowing that it's easy to take each other for granted in the

daily grind. Every six months or so, they revisit their vows and talk about what they mean. "Also, every once in a while, we have knock-down, drag-out fights and that's healthy too, as long as you don't say anything really mean," says Susie, channeling a little of her *Curb* character.

Susie's travel schedule also keeps the relationship fresh. She has to fly to California for weeks at a time for filming. "Being apart is good," says Susie. "I like missing him. It keeps the heat and the passion."

Though they might have liked to have found each other earlier, meeting in their late 40s had its advantages. With age comes wisdom. "It's easier to commit when you're older," says Jim. "You understand what that means better. You know the pitfalls."

And some things become less important with age, adds Susie. "Now sowing my wild oats means lowering my cholesterol." ❊

Judy Collins & Louis Nelson | A Lovely Discovery

JUDY AND LOUIS ARE A STRIKING COUPLE, as pleasing to the eyes as Judy's crystal-clear voice is to the ears. On this February afternoon, they are sitting on a plush couch in a suite at the Carlyle Hotel. Judy is in her fifth season there, doing a month-long show; the night before, she had included the number "Somewhere Over The Rainbow" in her repertoire.

Dressed in black, with a long white cardigan, Judy has long, silver hair that flows down her back. Louis has a gray lion's mane that extends past his shoulders and a full beard. Both have blue eyes that are set off by their whitened locks.

A mutual friend suggested that the two meet in 1978—inviting them both to a fundraiser in Manhattan celebrating the Equal Rights Amendment. It was held at the Ginger Man—which had been appropriately renamed the "Ginger Person" for the evening. She was 38 and he was 40.

That is when they met, says Louis, but not when their fates became set in stone. That happened a few months later on July 10 when they had their first real date. Louis had made dinner reservations at his favorite restaurant—now closed—Orsini's on 56th Street. "I was sitting there waiting for Judy," says Louis, who is wearing a dark gray suit over a black, mock-turtleneck, with a burst of color in the form of a teal pocket square. "She walked down the aisle, saw me, tilted her head and smiled." He remembers it vividly.

They talked for hours, until the waiters were ready to throw them out. "We haven't been apart since," says Judy. "We had a whole lot to talk about. You suddenly meet somebody and feel like you can talk about anything that ever happened to you."

"And we're still telling each other stories—33 years later," says Louis, an industrial designer whose varied projects include the covers of some of Judy's albums, the Korean War Memorial at the National Mall, the "Nutrition Facts" label for the FDA, and the restaurant at the Statue of Liberty.

When they met, Louis was not looking for a relationship. "But sometimes you have no control over those things," he says. "Right away, we were just together. You just know."

Their wedding rings have April 16th inscribed inside—the date of their first dinner. "That's when the magic happened. It was stamped on our lives from that moment on," says Collins.

The wedding did not happen, though, until 18 years after that first date. They lived together in an apartment on the Upper West Side, but marriage did not seem necessary. Both had been married before, Judy, once—"disastrously"—and Louis, twice.

"We were very happy and committed to each other and involved in each other's lives. We didn't feel any urgency," says Judy.

In 1993, though, Louis went into the hospital with acute appendicitis. As he lay in the hospital bed with tubes everywhere, Judy started worrying about the lack of legal authority she had if papers needed to be signed. As Louis awoke from a Demerol fog, she said anxiously that she thought they should get married.

"Getting married won't keep me from dying," he replied, before passing out again.

They married on April 16, 1996, the three-year delay due to the difficulty nailing down a date with their busy schedules. They meant for the wedding to be a small, family-only affair, but the guest list for the ceremony at St. John the Divine's Cathedral swelled to 500 people—"From Madeline Albright on," says Louis.

For Judy, this was an impressive evolution. Before meeting Louis, she had spent 15 years among a "cult of therapists" called the Sullivanians. "They did not believe in monogamy, marriage, commitment, and insisted kids should not be brought up by their parents," says Collins. Her therapist encouraged her to skip her father's funeral. "They thought that the family and commitment contributed to the dysfunction of a personality and hindered artistic growth in people. Coming full-circle from that has been kind of miraculous."

She doesn't look back on that period with regret. In fact, she's writing an autobiographical book that will touch on it: *Judy Blue Eyes: Sex, Drugs, Rock and Roll and the Music That Changed a Generation.* It did not ruin her life, but it does seem unfathomable to her now to have once conceived of commitment as something negative and unnatural.

"When I met Louis, I realized, 'Oh this is how it's meant to be.' If you find the person who's right for you, you're supposed to get into it and enjoy it," she says.

Before getting married, they worried that it might change their very beautiful relationship. And it did.

"Things did change. It wasn't immediately apparent but there was this new subliminal, untouchable feeling," says Louis. "We had an extraordinary relationship over 18 years—together almost constantly, we talked about everything and anything. We knew how we would share our lives—everything separate but equal. But there's something that happened a few months after being married. Something was different and I couldn't put my finger on what it was."

Judy felt the same way. They solved the mystery in an unlikely place—at the movie theater in 1998, seeing *Six Days and Seven Nights*, starring Harrison Ford and Anne Heche, as a ne'er-do-well pilot and hard-charging New York executive who get marooned on a desert island together. There was a moment in the film that resonated, when Ford's character says that he doesn't feel alone anymore. "It was the smartest part of the work," says Louis, who had an epiphany. "After marrying Judy, I didn't feel alone anymore."

"It's a strange thing that it came only after the wedding," says Judy. "I think it's the ritual of it—the bonding ceremony performed by the priest, the discussion between the two of you about the legal aspects and each other's finances, and the celebration with your family and friends."

"It resonates. It's ancient," she continues. "For us, at our age, marriage wasn't about having children or progeny. It was about emotional commitment. Something shifted—a strong, powerful, unseen force—that indicated that this is okay, that this is a safe place to be emotionally. And there's a different tranquility when you have that kind of emotional security. I felt that security in our relationship, but the wedding sealed it."

They laugh at the idea that a romantic comedy helped them to discover this. "We always cry at Harrison Ford movies," says Judy. "But it was probably the worst movie he was ever in," says Louis. "The worst piece of junk," adds Judy.

Sometimes we find enlightenment in the strangest places. ❋

Jerry Stiller & Anne Meara | Laugh Lines

WHEN JERRY STILLER was deciding on a name for his autobiography, he settled on *Married to Laughter: A Love Story Featuring Anne Meara.* The book starts not with his birth (that's in Chapter 2) but with a recounting of the first time Jerry met Anne. It was in an agent's waiting room in New York in 1953. The young actors were auditioning for stage work. Angel-faced Anne was wearing Mary Chess perfume and seemed sort of puritanical, writes Jerry. She went into the agent's office and came out minutes later, crying, saying the man had chased her around the room. Jerry offered to take her to coffee to console her. He was relieved she didn't order food as he was on a struggling actor's budget. ("Broke," he explains.)

When he offered to get the check, Anne replied, "Forget the check. Just stick some silverware in your pocket and let's get the hell out of here." Jerry loved that.

When they bumped into each other again a few weeks later, Anne invited him over to her Greenwich Village apartment for spaghetti. "Long story short. We got married six months later," says Jerry. Jerry was 26 and Anne 24.

Having lunch at Michael's in midtown, the famous couple, now in their 80s, can't help but attract the attention of passersby, who stare in from the sidewalk or stop by on their way out of the restaurant. Two newscasters visit the table and remark, "These two are comedic royalty." A former Republican congressman stops by to say he loves their work, but is shooed away by Anne. "Politics is dirtier than show business," she exclaims.

She and Jerry have been in the business since launching a comedy routine called Stiller & Meara that was honed at the Phase II in a Greenwich Village coffee house run by David Gordon, got picked up by *The Ed Sullivan Show,* and continues today as a weekly web series on Yahoo! during which they riff on subjects in the news. Along the way, they've both acted in plays and movies, with Jerry Stiller perhaps best-known for his loud, irascible turn as Frank Costanza on *Seinfeld* and the cellar-dwelling Arthur Spooner on *King of Queens.* They famously acted as spokespeople for Blue Nun, with their humorous commercials causing sales of the wine to spike. They also have two children, Amy and Ben, who are both performers. Their son, Ben Stiller, produces their Yahoo show.

"Both of our kids give us 'nachas,'" says Jerry, explaining that it's a Yiddish word meaning *blessings.* "While having kids and even when pregnant, Anne never stopped working. She was on *Sullivan* a few weeks after Ben was born. In a way, both were in Mommy's tummy when we were on *Sullivan.* We weren't spring chickens when we started to click. And we didn't want to stop."

Anne, wearing a gray vest over a black sweater and green dangly earrings, uses a dropper to add heart medicine to her tea. "I had open heart surgery. Too much smoking," she says. "I had a cow thing put in."

While Jerry is earnest this afternoon, Anne is full of one-liners. When she orders the roast chicken, she asks the waiter to swap out the "frites" for mashed potatoes. "Because I'm very blue collar," she says.

When asked about the meaning of commitment, Anne becomes serious, though. "No one knows the answer to that question," she says. "It's in process all the time."

In his book, Jerry discusses the stress on their relationship from their professional struggles. "Our relationship was great on stage, when the act came off well," says Anne.

In the early days of their marriage, a fight—the exact cause of which has been forgotten—led them to decide to split. "The fight seemed to spring out of the realization that our lives were going nowhere," writes Jerry in his book. "The question was, who would leave whom, and what would become of our kittens, Squeaky and Sniffles? There was nothing else to be divided."

They trekked to a friend's house where Anne planned to move temporarily, but after sitting down with the friend for coffee, wound up laughing together and making up. Their shared humor has helped them get through many obstacles over the years. It is the glue that helps hold their commitment in place. And their later professional triumphs helped too.

They both light up when talking about their first sketch on *The Ed Sullivan Show.* Anne played a newscaster interviewing Jerry, playing Mister Jonah, an old Jewish man visiting his daughter in Florida who, while swimming in the ocean, gets swallowed by a whale.

"Then what did you do?" asks Anne, launching into the routine.

"I sat down. The waiter came over…" replies Jerry.

"The waiter?"

"The maitre'd. He asked what I wanted to order."

"To order?"

"And I said, I'm in a whale. I'm not going to get Chinese. I'll have the fish."

The rhythm of their comedy routine is inseparable from that of their normal conversations, as when Anne talks about her conversion from Catholicism to Judaism after marrying Jerry. "I converted, but personally, I don't much care for religion," she says.

"What do you mean you don't care for religion?" he asks.

"I didn't say anything about spirituality, I feel very strongly about spirituality," she replies.

"You made Seders and we go to Yom Kippur," he protests. "Remember when we had Rodney Dangerfield over for our Seder and he helped his kids Brian and Melanie find the Afikomen."

"You fast on Yom Kippur! You fast," she corrects him.

"Yeah, and you fasted," he replies, triumphant.

Anne returns to commitment, and this time tries to come up with an answer for its meaning. "Commitment is another word for promise," she says. "You do what you do in your life, and you try to be connected to what you believe in and what you both believe in. You try to keep your promise. That's all." ✻

Jennifer & Catherine "Cat" Cora
There Are No Other Options

AMERICA'S FIRST FEMALE IRON CHEF is "Cat" to the world, but is Cathy to her partner, Jennifer. They met in 1999 at a ski lodge in Tahoe, sitting at adjacent tables at a World Tribe reggae concert.

Both were living in the Bay Area at the time and were visiting the lodge with friends. Jennifer, then 28, was a nanny working for a family, and Cat was 32. "Cathy was just a chef," says Jennifer.

It was before Cat wrote her three cookbooks, fusing foods from her Greek heritage and Southern upbringing into simple recipes; before she became a regular star on the Food Network; and before she made history in 2005 by becoming the first female challenger on *Iron Chef America*.

"We just hit it off," says Cat, her voice thick with a Mississippi accent. "We saw each other every night for seven months until we moved in together. That was it. We just both knew."

In 2001, they had a marriage ceremony in Napa Valley with their friends and family. Both sets of parents walked them down the aisle.

"That was our ceremony," says Cat. The couple did not rush to have a legal ceremony in the brief window in 2010 when same-sex marriages were being administered by the state. They feared that it could undermine the legal protections that they currently have through their domestic partnership as the controversy over the legitimacy of same-sex marriages continues to be debated in the courts. "We have all our trusts and wills in each other's names. We're as married as we can possibly be without the papers," says Cat.

"It's sad that we're still, in this day and age, fighting for basic civil rights for couples," continues Cat. "We're Americans. We're citizens of this country and we pay taxes."

"And we love each other," adds Jennifer. "Other couples are together for a week, married for six months and divorced. We've been together for over a decade."

Cat and Jennifer say they have a motto for their commitment: "There are no other options." They are resolved to be focused on each other and not think of other paths that could be taken.

"Once you open up the door to other options, you're screwed," says Cat. "Through thick and thin, up and down, hills and valleys, we're committed to working for each other and our family every day, in terms of changing and evolving together and encouraging each other's growth. We support each other being the best we can be in life."

On a Thursday morning, the Southern California–based couple is on speakerphone in their minivan after having dropped their four sons off at school. Wearing workout attire, they're planning to have breakfast together before going to the gym.

"We knew from the beginning that we both wanted to have kids," says Cat. After their 2001 ceremony, they started talking to adoption experts and to doctors about artificial insemination.

"We both wanted to carry but we were also looking into adoption," says Cat. The adoption route wound up being incredibly frustrating due to biases against same-sex couples. So they settled on in vitro fertilization, choosing one anonymous donor to provide the sperm for all of their children.

Jennifer carried their first two sons, now 7 and 3; they used one of her eggs for the first pregnancy and one of Cat's for the second. In 2009, they made headlines when they were pregnant at the same time. Cat was carrying a baby from Jennifer's embryo, and Jennifer had been implanted with both of their eggs, so that the biological mother would be unknown.

"We're committed to each other and our family," says Cat. "For us, commitment means we're together. It's us against the world."

Talking about their children raises some of the frustrations they feel around the legality of same-sex marriage. "It's bad that, though we have children together, we have to get a lawyer and adopt our own kids. We have to adopt our own children," emphasizes Cat. "That's just one example of why Proposition 8 [the California Marriage Protection Act, that limits recognition of marriage to only that between a man and a woman] is so frustrating and why it's important to allow couples to get married."

Cat's work requires that she travel about a third of every year. That can be challenging for them, as it's hard for Cat to leave the family and it demands that Jennifer stay home to take care of the children. "It takes determination and perseverance. It's not easy to reestablish our connection and commitment to each other every time I come home," says Cat. "It's not all sugar-coated. There are challenges. But we're committed to working through it."

After all, there are no other options. ☀

April Gornik & Eric Fischl | A Work in Progress

ART OPENINGS IN MANHATTAN can be long, drawn-out affairs. As the hands of the clock were creeping toward 11 p.m. at a Friday night dinner accompanying a gallery show, Eric and April ate their plates of rice, leaving before the servers could come around with ladles of curry. They had a two-hour drive to make to their sprawling compound of a home in the Hamptons.

Neither got much sleep that night, but April got less. In the early hours of the morning, she heard their two Bengal cats playing unusually loudly. So she went upstairs to investigate and wound up rescuing a mouse by catching it under a glass, though only after it ran across her foot. She took it out into the woods and gave its head a little rub before letting it go.

One of the cats sits in her arms now, his emerald gaze and tiger stripes complementing her light-blue eyes and long auburn hair. The stunning cats were a birthday gift from Eric. "As an animal welfare activist, I feel a little guilty about our buying cats," she says. But it seems like only tigers would feel comfortable wandering through their high-ceiling home, with its split-level floors, walls of windows, and Zen-like recessed pools of water.

Occasionally, the cats wander into Eric and April's studios, mirror images of one another, flanking the front of the house. In Eric's studio are canvases of nudes, a sculpture of two males attached at the waist, and the lingering smell of cigar smoke. Across their front walk, April's studio seems to let in more sun, bathing her light-enthused landscape paintings with golden rays.

The two celebrated artists met in Canada in 1976 at the Nova Scotia College of Art and Design; April was a student in her early 20s, and Eric a teacher in his late 20s. "April was the most beautiful girl up there," says Eric, whose uniform of black clothing is interrupted only by a pair of green-striped socks and his shock of white-silver hair that is standing up in all directions. "That was back when they didn't pay you much to teach. But there were other perks."

"Evil perks," April adds, laughing. She was reluctant to date Eric at first, but not because he was a professor. "I was interested in conceptual art, so I was in the studio art program. Eric was in the more passé painting program. It took a while because I didn't initially want to fraternize with someone from the painting program."

They overcame their artistic differences and moved to New York together in 1978. They started out in Chelsea and then took a big loft apartment in Tribeca, which was not the hot spot it is today. "It was really bleak then," says April.

They were two struggling New York artists and there were difficult times. "We're artists so we're professional self-torturers," says April. "Sometimes it was great and sometimes it was frustrating, because we were jealous of each other."

"Artists are jealous of every other artist. They can have the whole world in their hand and still be jealous when another artist is having a show. It's absurd," says Eric. "Sometimes it was almost a deal breaker. We had to take it a problem at a time."

Of course, there are upsides to sharing a professional passion. "It's a challenging thing to be in the same field, but it's also deeply satisfying," says April. "One of the most fun things we can do possibly do is to go to an art show together and talk about our ideas. It's so much fun."

Beyond the professional pressure of trying to find success in New York's art world, Eric and April are "emotionally embattled people," who had had tragic home lives and struggled to open themselves up to one another. "We both gave each other space, to feel safe," says April. "We gave one another room to be whoever we needed to be. We had a really intuitive sense of that need in one another."

Rather than forcing the commitment, they say they drew it out of one another—over a very long period of time. They did not get married until 20 years later, in 1998.

They had a small ceremony in Rome, "the eternal city," with just a dozen friends. "It was time," says Eric. "I was turning 50. For me somehow, it was unsupportable to continue in a gray area of the relationship."

"There was some meaning to that action that hadn't existed before," says April. "We had been through a lot, as people do in 22 years. But before, marriage seemed like someone else's idea of what we should do. And at that point, it seemed like our idea of what we should do."

It was not easy logistically. There were many trips paid to the State Department and to the Italian embassy to cut through the red tape around having a civil ceremony in another country. The wedding was held in a little farmhouse near Circus Maximus.

"Marriage is a profound statement, a public statement," says Eric. "We had certainly in 22 years made private commitments, but because they were private, they seemed breakable. When you get married, you're publicly stating something that can be shared with everyone. It seemed clarifying."

So now they are committed to one another, before their friends, the Italian and U.S. governments, and the world. What does that commitment mean to them?

"Commitment is trust and intimacy. Intimacy is probably the most difficult thing to get comfortable with," says Eric. "Intimacy is a deep sharing, a place where boundaries merge. It's always a scary place."

Most people have a deep fear of exposing their vulnerabilities, but that is at the heart of intimacy. "Being able to be vulnerable with someone you love is the glue that holds you together and is also the most terrifying thing," says April.

Eric and April tend to use the word *love* instead of the word *commitment* in talking about their relationship and their work. "The nature of being an artist is you're asking for love and looking for love on a relatively constant basis," says Eric.

"I don't know if I relate to the word *commitment*," April says. "I relate to trust, intimacy and loyalty. And I relate to the idea of trying to really be there for and with the person you love. But it seems like it has to be a fluid thing. People change and grow. It has to be fluid and in motion and active."

"It's still a work in progress," adds April, as if their relationship is a painting not yet complete.

"Oh certainly. Marriage doesn't end something," says Eric. "It begins a new chapter." ※

Daryl & Steven Roth | Choosing Commitment

DARYL AND STEVEN ROTH DESCRIBE THEMSELVES as "serious people." They are one of New York's consummate power couples, with her success in the arts and his in business. Steven is the chairman of Vornado Realty Trust, and Daryl is a prolific producer on Broadway and off-Broadway, including six Pulitzer Prize–winning plays. "Art meets commerce," says Daryl of their pairing.

Steven's spacious corner office, 46 floors up on Seventh Avenue, provides a stunning view of Manhattan. If one wants a closer view, there's a telescope set up before one of the walls of windows. Taking in the view, like the eyes of Doctor T. J. Eckleburg in *The Great Gatsby*, is a massive self-portrait by Chuck Close, a birthday present from Daryl to Steven. It hangs on the wall behind Steven's large wooden work desk, which is covered with stacks of paper, and a placard sign that says, "Trouble is opportunity."

What does it mean to be serious people? Often it means long nights, for one. Daryl stops by Steven's office one evening at 6 p.m. for an hour visit knowing they'll both be working that evening. Afterward, Steven will continue a series of meetings and Daryl will go to her theater for an encouraging pep talk with a young actor, nervous about starring in his first Broadway production. They both care deeply about their work.

Their seriousness and practicality is reflected in the story of their initial courtship. After meeting Daryl in 1968, Steven's roommate set them up on a blind date. Daryl, an avowed dog lover, had a test for all of her suitors on the first date. When they dropped her off at home, she would ask them if they would like to walk her dog with her. Unlike almost everybody else, Steven declined. "He said, 'Absolutely not. I don't want to walk your dog,'" recalls Daryl. "And that was the end of that."

She didn't see him again. "Because I figured someone who doesn't love dogs is not for me." But they reconnected a year later when Daryl included Steven in her holiday card

mailings. He called her, they went out and were married in May 1969, three months later. "I had been engaged and broken it off in that year," said Daryl. "And I didn't want to go through an engagement again. I figured we love each other, if we want to get married, let's just do it," and it felt very right.

They had their first child, a daughter, two years later and their son three years after that. It all seems to have happened in a lockstep manner; their determination to commit to one another and start a family similar to their determination in their professional spheres. "When I first met Steven, he had no money, he was just starting his business, and he was working 24 hours a day, seven days a week," says Daryl. "He is a self-made man and I have great respect for that." Since he had traditional notions of a wife who would take care of the family, Daryl stopped working when she had her daughter. "My family was my career," she says, "And I loved my family and my home, so I was content at that time."

She tilts her head to the side as she thinks about commitment.

"Commitment means making a moral, heartfelt, and cerebral decision to be loyal to someone and go through various stages of life together," Daryl says. "It is a deeper commitment when you have children, and it was important to both of us to have a very stable and loving home. Our commitment to each other had a lot to do with the family unit."

As the children got older, Daryl wanted to return to work and pursue her love of theater, and so, 23 years ago, she produced her first show off-Broadway. The time was right.

"You're going to share what life gives you: good, bad, and indifferent. The beauty of being together with someone for a long time is that you will grow and change and both have different interests and shared interests," says Daryl. "Part of being committed to one another is allowing each other to find their own way and to feel supported and encouraged, and not to feel as though anything undermines the relationship. If the commitment is primary and foremost in your mind, you feel permitted to grow."

Steven enters his office wearing a dark pinstripe suit, paisley tie, and a light blue shirt. He says hello in a gravelly voice, and takes a seat. He describes commitment in more concrete and almost business-like terms. "Commitment is a synonym for partnership. But there's a romance side. An intellectual side. A companionship side," says Steven. "And a pride."

Though Steven originally objected to his wife's working, he now looks at that impulse as "stupid, old-fashioned, and destructive," and swells with pride at talking about what

Daryl has achieved and who and what she brings to the table. "Think about it," says Steven. "During the day, I dig ditches and at night, I have dinner with Edward Albee. How else could I have done that?"

In talking about their 41 years of marriage, Daryl and Steven like to point to their accomplishments in the professional sphere as evidence of the strength of their commitment. It is the foundation upon which their lives are built. "We both have great love and respect for one another and share this deep sense of family. Even when things are not going well—and all relationships have challenges—we've chosen to stay together," says Daryl. "We are devoted to one another; it's a very conscious choice and we've made it."

On a side table is a photo of them with their family including their four grandchildren taken at a Vornado picnic. They also have two Lowchen dogs, not in the photo. Though he was not in the room when Daryl brought up his aversion to dog-walking, Steven brings it up now as a measurable sign of his commitment. He has softened and actually admits he likes it when Leo and Lucy come and cuddle up by his side. ※

Charles & Phyllis Rosenthal | A Valuable Investment

CHARLES AND PHYLLIS' ROMANCE BLOOMED from the seeds of a consolation date.

In the early 1960s, Phyllis was working at an advertising agency in Manhattan and dating one of Charles' Wall Street colleagues. An Argentine citizen, she used to go back to Buenos Aires in the winters to avoid New York's nasty weather and to be with her family. Her then-boyfriend was supposed to come visit her there with plans to meet her family and propose. But at the last minute, a wedding gone wrong in an episode of the Western *Gunsmoke* spooked him; he canceled the trip and he and Phyllis broke up.

When she returned to New York that spring, Charles took her out to cheer her up. "He was going to console me," says Phyllis. "But I brought a flower," adds Charles. It's easy to imagine him offering his sympathies to Phyllis 48 years ago with his warm, brown eyes, and her falling for him instead.

They describe the ensuing relationship as "whirlwind." That first date in March 1963 was followed by a City Hall wedding in June and an official ceremony with friends and family in Switzerland in July. Why so fast?

"We were pretty old for those days," says Charles, who was 27. Phyllis, curled up on the couch in a black hooded sweatshirt and jeans, prefers not to reveal her age, but had been out of college for a few years, which was unusual for women then. Most got married right after graduation. "I went to Bryn Mawr, though," says Phyllis. "The motto was, 'Only our failures marry.'"

Charles, dressed more formally in a checkered shirt with elephants on a red tie, has recently gotten home from the investing firm, First Manhattan Co., where he is a senior managing director. A full head of stately white hair sets off skin tan from a love of the outdoors, which is one way that his and Phyllis' tastes diverge.

He loves skiing and tennis—on a shelf behind his computer chair is a photo of Charles with Roger Federer, displayed prominently along with photos of their daughter and grandchildren. Phyllis prefers the theater and art galleries to sports. Charles likes to go out to their house in the East Hampton to go on nature walks, while Phyllis is happy to be confined to Manhattan.

"If you told Phyllis that she had to stay on Madison Avenue for the rest of her life, and she couldn't even go to Third Avenue, she'd be very happy," says Charles.

Phyllis seems nearly as committed to New York as she is to Charles. She visited for the first time with her mother when she was 15 and fell in love with the city. Going to the United States became like "going to Mecca." As a person, Phyllis describes herself as "very consistent, constant and directed."

"And New York was my direction," she says. Being from Brooklyn, a life in New York suited Charles as well. Just as Phyllis can't imagine being anywhere but New York, Charles can't imagine his life without Phyllis.

"As I get older, I don't know how I would live without her," says Charles. "Commitment is a way of life."

In seeking to define the meaning of commitment, Phyllis sought the help of Google. "These are the results that struck me," she says, listing them off. "Responsibility, tolerance, loyalty, support, open-mindedness, trust, dedication to a long-term course of action."

In seeking the meaning within herself, her description is more elemental. "You're bound and you're bound," she says. "You don't waver."

Charles and Phyllis think that commitment might be underappreciated these days. Phyllis cites a cartoon she saw in the *New York Post* that morning, with a woman asking whether marriage is obsolete. Her comic companion responds, "No, I'm perfectly happy to be in a monotonous relationship." She replies, "It's monogamous, not monotonous!"

Being together as long as Charles and Phyllis have been, they say there is monotony, of course. Some nights, Charles listens to music in one room and Phyllis watches TV in another. A couple has patterns and there is a comfort in that—as Charles is reminded every time he travels for work. "When I'm away, I know I have a home and a person to come back to," says Charles. "If I didn't, life would be very sad."

Perhaps because he has spent his life as an investment advisor, Charles talks about their commitment in terms of its long-term value. "When you look back on your life, you realize that you've gathered all these material things. They get worn out, and you get new ones, and they get worn out again," he says. "But the commitment lasts. It doesn't wear out." ❋

Bryan Batt & Tom Cianfichi | Madly in Love

ON *MAD MEN,* Bryan Batt played an art director in a 1950s advertising firm who must keep his sexuality a secret given the social mores of the time. In real life, Bryan kept his sexual orientation a secret as well—or so he thought—until he settled into a stable relationship with a fellow actor, Tom Cianfichi.

Bryan and Tom met in Akron, Ohio in 1989 while working on a dinner theater production of *Evita.* The female actresses on the set wondered aloud to Tom which of them the charming Bryan had taken a liking to. Tom thought it might be him, and he was right.

"Tom was the first guy that, when I met him, I thought to myself, 'Oh, this is what it's like. I can have love in my life,'" says Bryan. "I didn't know. I didn't have any role models. I didn't know any gay couples. I thought I was doomed to a lonely life, a sad existence. And then I met him, and I realized that feeling of love that everyone was talking about."

That feeling blossomed into a lasting relationship. "'Commitment.' So many people are so afraid of that word, but it's one of the most comforting feelings in the world," says Bryan.

Bryan, who leads a rather peripatetic life, is on the phone from New Orleans, where he and Tom have a home in the Garden District. He is home to celebrate their 22nd anniversary (on April 1st). Bryan grew up in the Big Easy and is devoted to supporting the culture of the city: he had spent the past week performing in a benefit production of *Love Letters* with Patricia Clarkson to try to save a 95-year-old theater, and is working on a book about New Orleans style. Tom, originally from Pennsylvania, has adopted Louisiana as his full-time home. While Bryan travels frequently—to Los Angeles for filming and to New York, where they also have an apartment, for stage work—Tom spends the bulk of his time in New Orleans, having given up acting to focus on managing a delightful décor boutique, Hazelnut, that he and Bryan opened there.

"What keeps us going is that we're very different. I love going out. I love parties," says Bryan. "Tom is content to sit at home and relax, and hang with the dog and have friends over. We complement each other."

When the two first met over two decades ago, they had something in common: they were both still in the closet. Neither had told their families that they were gay. After dating for a year—often long distance as their acting careers took them to various cities—Bryan was cast in a Broadway production, and they decided to move into an apartment together in New York. Initially, they let their families assume that they were just roommates.

Bryan was most worried about telling his brother, who he describes as an "open-minded Republican." In 1993, after he and Tom had been together for four years, Bryan's brother asked if he was gay.

"I thought he was going to have a problem with it, and was afraid to tell him. But when I told him, he responded, 'Oh, thank God. I thought you weren't getting any,'" says Bryan, laughing. The rest of their family members were similarly supportive. "We were very lucky. Some families are not as accepting."

Bryan and Tom's commitment to one another was initially a very private one, due to this secrecy. Bryan still values that privacy—now without the burden of secrecy—given his high-profile career.

"Relationships are an interpersonal thing," says Bryan. Being in the public eye too much—having your relationship documented on camera and scrutinized in the press—can make commitment harder, he says. "There are some things you want to keep private. I don't know how some celebrities deal with it, with paparazzi hanging out in trees—catching couples in a fight or having matrimonial difficulties. Who doesn't? Everyone has problems."

Still, there is a public gesture of commitment that Tom and Bryan might like to make: getting married. They were going to have a ceremony in California when same-sex marriage was legalized there, but Bryan's mother was very ill. They are very close; Bryan wrote a touching memoir about her, published in 2010, titled *She Ain't Heavy, She's My Mother*. They wanted her to be there, so they decided to wait.

"We had no idea Prop 8 was going to be overturned," says Bryan. Sadly, his mother has since passed away.

Tom and Bryan are cheered though by the number of states that are starting to pass laws giving same-sex couples the right to marry. "For so many years, we never dreamed it would happen. Now that it's a reality, it's so enchanting and reaffirming. I'm just thrilled."

Some straight couples are together for years but don't feel the need to be married. Bryan won't say for sure what he and Tom will do, but they know they'd prefer to be able to make the decision in their hometown. In 2004, Louisiana passed a law banning same-sex marriages and civil unions. "I don't think that I should have to travel outside of my city, my state to have such a basic right to be acknowledged," says Bryan. Given their love and support for the city, it seems especially tragic that the city won't legally recognize their bond.

The state may not affirm their relationship, but they do—every day, to each other.

"What I love about our commitment is that we wake up and there is no piece of paper. We don't have a legal binding ceremony or document that keeps us together," says Bryan. "Every morning, we wake up and make that decision to be together. And we've been making that decision every day for the last 22 years." ※

Bruce & Barbara Berger | Bending Prevents Breaking

BRUCE AND BARBARA are able to narrow their list of life-long priorities to just three items: kids, art, and the outdoors. "In that order," says Bruce.

All three are evident on a Sunday morning in November in their Manhattan apartment. Bruce has recently flown back from their full-time residence in Aspen, Colorado, where he is in the midst of preparations to open a new mountainside restaurant. He walks in with an armful of groceries for an afternoon visit from their kids and grandchildren, while Barbara, in a short black sweater dress and tights, is offering a visitor a spontaneous tour of their fabulous art collection.

One of their pieces hangs not on the wall but in it: a concave collection of circles scooped out of the plaster—"Like an architectural space that has collapsed in on itself," says Bruce—based on a mold from contemporary artist Ricky Albende. Its curves are subtly echoed in the drapery of the clothing of a Greek hermaphrodite lounging on a pedestal nearby and the curves of a Robert Mapplethorpe calla lily. Antiquity and modernity rest comfortably near one another in the Bergers' home.

As Bruce, wearing a black turtleneck and a short white beard, walks into the kitchen with the groceries, he asks Barbara why she hasn't taken out the trash. A black plastic bag slumps dejectedly in the corner of the room. She laughs. It's another modern sculpture—a patinated bronze that looks incredibly realistic.

While they laugh easily together, a conversation about commitment can turn tense when the subject of their new restaurant in Aspen comes up. It was Bruce's idea, and Barbara is being dragged along for the ride. She's used to that, though.

The two have known each other since childhood—initially as neighbors in Long Island, New York. "We met when Barbara was 4 years old," says Bruce. "I knew she was the one instantly," he jokes. They haven't been together since their toddler days, but they were high school sweethearts. Her family moved a few towns over, but Bruce crashed Barbara's confirmation party in 1954 and they started dating.

After they got married in 1960, Bruce pursued a career in real estate and construction. His work took them first to Vermont—"I dragged Barbara to live on a farm for five years," says Bruce—and then to Colorado. "It was whither thou goest in those days," says Barbara, who let her husband plot their life course. She grew to love the mountains and raising their two children with easy access to the great outdoors. "The family that hikes and skis together stays together," quips Bruce.

Barbara was a schoolteacher for a short time, but it didn't suit her. She instead devoted herself to raising their son and daughter. "But Bruce didn't like being married to a housewife who recited 'Mary Had A Little Lamb' every night, so he encouraged me to go into business. He believed in me and knew I could do something very special," says Barbara. In 1972, she launched a career as an art consultant. She proved adept at it, initially buying pieces for corporations and law firms in the 1970s and 1980s, and then taking on individual private clients.

"I was encouraged to expand myself as a human being," says Barbara. "We have a commitment to making the other person feel good about their life. We care about the other person realizing their life's dreams."

Even when that dream seems like a bad idea. Bruce, who has loved cooking all of his life, plans to open an American bistro in Aspen this winter. "I tried to talk him out of it because I don't think it's wise timing," says Barbara, who worries about it interfering with their ability to travel, see art, and visit with their children and grandchildren. "I was very angry about the potential intrusion on our life's plan."

"It was the first test of our commitment in 50 years," says Bruce. "This was the first time she wasn't immediately willing to follow me."

Bruce told her that he planned to name the restaurant B.B.'s Kitchen, using Barbara's nickname. She objected, but he insisted, saying "B.B." were his initials too. (Incidentally, B.B.'s Kitchen opened in December 2010, and is doing very well.)

Many a relationship benefits from one person being willing to bend. Over the course of their lives, it seems that Barbara has been most willing to do that. She eventually agreed to do the interior design and art program for B.B.'s. "Once I realized I couldn't talk him out of it, I knew I had to support him," says Barbara.

Supporting one other is at the foundation of their commitment. "For me, commitment has been Bruce pushing me to be the very best that I can be, and giving me the opportunity and space to excel as a person," says Barbara. She encourages Bruce in return. Now she'll be giving him the chance to excel as a restauranteur.

These two are always pushing each other to do greater things. For Barbara's 70th birthday in July, she requested that the two of them do a 14-mile hike across the Rockies from Aspen to Crested Butte, over a 13,000-foot pass. "I was determined," says Barbara. "Together we can accomplish anything—and we did."

"Commitment is ensuring that the other person is as happy as you are, and that each of you is maximizing your goals in life," says Bruce. ※

Evan Galen & Steve Novick
Certifiable Commitment

VISITORS TO EVAN AND STEVE'S airy Park Avenue apartment are greeted at the door by sculptures of a bunny emerging from a magician's hat with his own hat in hand, a bronzed bald eagle with wings spread, and a cow, peaking out from behind the eagle's pedestal. The only real animals in the house—their Havanese puppy, Bo, and his four-legged friend of the same breed from next door—race from room to room, past a roaring lion, a penguin under a piano, a bulldog, a manatee, miniature bunnies, and a pair of sheep.

"Do you want to see the one we shot in Maine?" asks Steve, going to the kitchen and pointing mischievously at the mounted head of a teddy bear. The visual prank does not detract from the loveliness of the apartment, which reflects the elegance of Evan's touch. Evan is a New York–based architect who designs the homes of celebrities and high-end residential clients.

Seated in their dark-wood-paneled library, Steve perches on the back of the couch, poking Evan. "Don't be so serious," Steve says, as they pose for a photo. "Don't do that face."

Steve, a retired advertising executive who just had his 70th birthday, is full of energy. He races around the apartment like their puppy, looking for somewhere new for them to pose. He sets them up in front of the lion. "I feel like a jerk," says Evan, 63. "We look like Siegfried and Roy."

Steve laughs, and it's obvious that they love to needle one another with a playfulness that belies the fact that they have been together for 37 years. They met at a dinner party at Pete's Tavern in Gramercy Park in 1973, and fell for each other quickly, moving in together a few months later.

Many people, especially young couples in the gay world, ask them about the secret of their relationship success. "A lot of it is luck," says Evan. "A lot of it is the intention to be in a relationship. And a lot of it is finding a person where you both think the other one is

terrific. You have to be very sure, though, right from the very beginning that your ethics and their ethics are on the same line on a million practical levels."

"Without that, there is no point to commitment. It's just a sham," Evan continues. "If your basic cores are at odds, it's never going to work no matter how much you pretend. And I think that's knowable very quickly—whether a person is in sync with how you think life should be."

While they share values, they're different in many other superficial ways. Steve is short. Evan is tall. Steve is wearing black-and-white Puma sneakers. Evan is in brown loafers. "Everything that he does, I do differently. Almost everything. I talk fast, he talks slowly. I stay up late, he goes to bed early," Steve says. "But it doesn't make any difference. When it comes to the fundamental issues of right and wrong and good and bad, the right thing to do, there's never a discussion. We're opposites, except in anything that has any real significance."

"We have a rule—either we both agree or we don't do it," Steve adds. Evan says this applies to his work as well. "I learned this in the design business with my clients. I always say, 'If one of you says no, we don't do it.' There's no discussion after that. Because in design you're always arguing."

One significant decision they made two years ago was to get married. They were attending a wedding in Los Angeles at the Bel Air Hotel in September 2008. It was their first gay wedding and it was going to be a lavish one—fancy food, white rose petals on the aisle, "every Bridezilla's dream," says Steve.

They had wondered for some time about getting married themselves. "It's pointless right now until there's law that upholds the marriage, so the rest of it is all just symbolic which is nice if you're 27, 28, 29, or 30, but if you're our age, after 35 years, it's not going to make any significant difference in our lives," said Steve. But their accountant suggested it was a good idea for technical reasons—for handling taxes, their estates, and having authority should one of them end up in the hospital—and that they should do it while it was legal in California, as it could become illegal (as it did soon thereafter).

They didn't want to outshine the groom and groom, so they did it quietly. When they arrived, they asked the concierge if it could be arranged. A testament to the Bel Air's customer service, he simply replied, "What time would you like it to take place?"

They spent the next day by the pool with their friends' wedding guests, and when the judge arrived in the afternoon, they slipped away quietly. The judge married them in their room, and then they ushered him out and went back to swimming.

Steve and Evan have been wearing wedding rings for decades, so they don't regard the California marriage as highly significant. "If it had any meaning, it would have meaning," said Steve. "If the government says yes, you're legally married, it would have meaning."

Given their ages, they have seen society's attitude toward being gay evolve, from something that was not mentioned at all to a growing acceptance, as states across the nation make legislative moves to recognize same-sex relationships and marriages.

"The wedding was fun and nice, but the meaning of it is debatable. What does that piece of paper mean after 35 years?" asks Steve. "We're not firebrands," adds Evan. "Like our friends who got married at the Bel Air—they are very involved in 'Don't Ask, Don't Tell' and gay marriage equality and are worried about the injustice of it all. But we're a generation before them, and the injustice of it seems to us just the way the world is."

Legislatures allowing gay marriage in Massachusetts, Connecticut, Iowa, Vermont, New Hampshire, and D.C., and the California courts overturning Proposition 8—a proposal to recognize marriage as only that between a man and a woman—are signs that the U.S. is changing. "It's a serious and important step forward in the evolution of our society just the way interracial marriage evolved in this country. Just the way women's rights evolved," says Steve. "There are important intellectual minds that think this is the wave of the future, that this is what's right—constitutionally and morally."

Same-sex marriage has cultural and political significance, but Evan and Steve's commitment goes far beyond that. "Commitment is as much unspoken, unwritten, as it is anything else," says Steve. "It's an inherent, ongoing quality of your life. It's not something you have to affirm with a certificate." Evan and Steve aren't even sure where their marriage certificate from California is.

"Commitment is a personal thing. It doesn't have to do with laws," says Evan. No matter what the law recognizes, these two see their commitment as taking priority over everything else. "In a deeply committed relationship, the relationship takes precedence over every other relationship. It's not like you have your family and then you have your relationship. Your relationship is your family. Your biological family becomes secondary," says Evan. "So when someone asks how long Steve and I have been together, my immediate thought is, 'my whole life.'" ※

Arnold Scaasi & Parker Ladd
Simple and Understated

ARNOLD AND PARKER'S APARTMENT high above the East River is dramatically decorated. The foyer features a stone floor and red walls hung with an early Leger and a tribal mask. A glimpse into a bathroom beneath a wooden spiral staircase reveals wallpaper of verdant green jungle print on a silver ground. Their living room yields a large Picasso and larger-than-life statues of two 13th-century "Chinese ladies," flanking a ceiling-high Louise Nevelson wall. A bust of Poseidon, silhouetted by floor-to-ceiling windows, appears to be pointing at the Queensboro Bridge, not far north of the building.

On side tables are Council of Fashion Designer award statuettes that Arnold has received (including a 1998 Lifetime Achievement Award) and photos of Arnold with a few of the women whose dresses he has designed, including Princess Di and Barbara Bush (who wrote a note: "With love to Arnold. I love my Scaasi.").

In discussing their relationship, though, Arnold and Parker are not very dramatic at all. They met in 1962 at a dinner party. "We liked each other very much and started to see each other," says Arnold. "If you care about someone, you commit to them. If you don't care, you don't commit."

They have continued to like each other for almost five decades. Parker, though, says he was not looking for a long-term relationship when they first met. Arnold had been in New York for 10 years at that point, having moved to Manhattan from France to work with Charles James. But Parker, who was working for Charles Scribner, was freshly arrived in New York, having moved there four months ago from California. He was not planning to make any serious attachments so soon.

"I met Arnold and it was summer. He was wearing a vest under his jacket and carrying gloves," says Parker. (Arnold says that, after Paris, "That's the way I dressed.") "And so

I thought, he's not threatening because he's going home to England, obviously. Nobody in New York wears gloves year-round."

A year later, Parker took the penthouse apartment above Arnold's duplex at 100 Central Park South. "A good way to shake down a relationship is not to live together, but in adjoining units," says Parker.

They did not move into their current shared apartment until 1989. "After 20 years, we thought we could throw the dice and be all right," says Ladd.

They are understated in describing their commitment—for them, it has been simple, fundamental, and even easy. "If you like someone, love someone, and care about them, and you keep seeing them, you're automatically committed," says Arnold. "Unless you suddenly don't like them anymore, and then you leave. It's matter of fact."

They speculate that their strong bond may be stronger due to being able to focus entirely on one another. "It may be that not having children makes it better. It means you're selfish and you can just think about each other," says Arnold.

They share the same values and the same likes. "That's the most important part in any couple," says Arnold. They don't share as much in the professional realm. "It helps that we don't have the same vocations. So there's never any professional competition. Books are my life. And fashion is his," says Ladd, though Arnold has dabbled in books, having authored memoirs, including *Women I Have Dressed (And Undressed!)*.

The only major friction they recall in their relationship came from their divergent belief systems. Ladd is a tall Vermonter. Arnold, who comes to Parker's shoulder, was raised Jewish in Montreal, reflected by a pin on his lapel which combines the Canadian and American flags. "We have different philosophies of life, in a minor way. I'm an agnostic. I believe there is no eternity. And he's much more optimistic," says Parker.

Basing their partnership in religion or in a sanction from the government might have been easier, says Parker. "It's more difficult when you have to keep it sotto voce. You can't just get up on a stage and get married."

Their commitment, instead, is rooted in the decades they've spent together. "I'm a committed person. If I like something, I remain committed. I happen to like Parker, so I remain committed," says Arnold. "It's just a fact of life. You don't have to go on for more than 40 years, but we did."

The same kind of commitment applies to their favorite breed of dogs. Over the course of those years, they have had 30 dogs, all Irish terriers, including their two current dogs, Henry and River. When they find something they like, they stick with it.

"The good motivation is that Arnold is never boring," adds Ladd. "So those 48 years have never been boring. I think it would be easier to uncommit if you get bored."

"By this time, I think it's too late," says Arnold. "I hope I'm not boring, but if I am, you're stuck with it." ※

Drs. Jerry Gliklich & Jane Salmon | Doing Good

THOUGH MARRIED FOR OVER THREE DECADES, Jane still thrills at the sight of her husband in his medical attire. "You look cute in your white coat," she says to Jerry when he drops by her research lab at the Hospital for Special Surgery in Manhattan.

The two met as students at Columbia Medical School in the early 1970s in a then-new program to train doctors in academic science. Jane was just 20 when she started the program, and its first female student; after meeting her at a wine tasting, Jerry, then 24, took it upon himself to be her mentor. That mentorship eventually evolved into a romantic relationship. "Since then, she's mentored me a lot," says Jerry, looking at his wife adoringly.

They married in 1976. Their friends thought them radical for exchanging vows at such a young age, while Jane's mother thought her daughter radical for not changing her last name. "My parents were very upset. Jerry and I had a joint checking account. My mother said, 'When you pay your electric or telephone bill, they'll think you're living in sin,'" recounts Jane, who preferred to keep the name that graced her diplomas. "I said, 'Don't worry about it. As long as I pay the bill, they'll be happy.'"

While Jerry went on to work with patients as a cardiologist, Jane concentrated on research, winning awards for her groundbreaking work on lupus. In her office hang paired paintings of Little Red Riding Hood and the wolf, a playful nod to her area of specialty.

In talking about their commitment, Jerry and Jane concentrate on the support they gave each other personally that allowed them to thrive professionally. Jane prides herself for being a role model for women who want to be wives, mothers and scientists—"and do all of them adequately," she adds.

"You have to juggle which becomes the priority at which moment in time. When our two sons were little, I was a mother more than anything else and Jerry worked very hard. And then when my kids got older and did a lot of sports—I didn't like sports—I became

more the scientist and Jerry was the supporter and spectator. He closed his office and went to wrestling and lacrosse matches."

"We take turns, we share," Jane continues. "We share everything but the cooking," Jerry adds, laughing.

Vivacious and petite, Jane tends to take the lead in conversation, with Jerry offering humor and elaboration in an Eastern European accent that reflects his growing up in Łódź, Poland. One of the many things these two have in common is a family history deeply impacted by World War II. Jane's parents were German refugees who fled to New York City. Jerry's were Polish concentration camp survivors. Coincidentally, their parents married on the same day in the same year, continents apart.

"Commitment means accepting all aspects of the other person," says Jane. "It's aligning yourself with the other person, finding common values, and understanding the other person's needs and enhancing that person's ability to satisfy himself or herself."

A significant part of that enhancement for these two has been to help each other become better doctors. Their passion for their work and their commitment to one another are intimately intertwined. Given his work with patients, Jerry coached Jane to improve her public speaking, so that she could explain her work to non-experts and secure funding for her research. "He de-jargonized me," she says. And if Jerry has a patient with heart disease who happens to have arthritis, he consults with his wife for advice on what to prescribe.

"We're do-gooders," says Jane. "We are both people who not only give to our patients and give to our institutions and give to our academic communities, but give to each other and help each other do that better."

Now that their sons are in their 20s and independent, Jerry and Jane focus on their work and on each other. A collage of postcards from far-flung countries decorates a memory board in Jane's lab—proof of the trips they now have the time to take together.

"Being committed is not always easy. For two people to live together a long time and not do each other in is not easy," says Jerry, lest the description of their do-gooder lives together seem too idyllic.

"You have to try to help your partner through their difficult times and your own difficult times together," he continues. "You have to be open to, interested in, and excited about the new avenues down which they seek to take you, and learn about and participate in the things that make them happy."

Ideally, their happiness becomes your own. ※

Danny & Audrey Meyer | Through Thick and Thin

DANNY MEYER FOUND HIS LOVE in restaurants—professionally and romantically. The man behind the award-winning Union Square Cafe, Gramercy Tavern and Eleven Madison Park, and long-line–inspiring Shake Shack sensation got his start as an apprentice at a New York restaurant called Pesca in 1984. Audrey Heffernan, a stage actress, was also working there as a waitress to pay her rent.

Metaphorically at the bottom step of his career, he was at the top of a staircase when he first met Audrey. Wearing her uniform of khakis, a Brooks Brother shirt and a tie, she was carrying ramekins of butter up from the basement of the stylish seafood restaurant. The door at the top of the stairs opened to reveal Pesca's owner standing with Danny. The mutual attraction was immediate.

"We now call it the stairway glance," says Audrey. "I noticed his eyes. They were warm, gentle, open, soft, and friendly."

Danny tried unsuccessfully to ask Audrey out several times, first throwing a Kentucky Derby party at his apartment for the sole purpose of seeing her outside of work. But she was going to be out of town for her brother's wedding. Then he asked her out on a date, but she came down with strep throat. "I was convinced these were just excuses, and I took it as rejection," says Danny.

So he showed up at Pesca one night on a date with an "older woman," and succeeded in his plan to make Audrey jealous. Soon thereafter, Audrey heard that Danny was heading to Europe for a four-month apprenticeship. "I hear you're moving to France," she said to him. He replied, "So I think you and I should probably go out on that date before I go."

On his last night of work at Pesca, they went to see "Noises Off" on Broadway, and then went restaurant-hopping. At the Odeon, he leaned across the table and kissed her.

"I borrowed a line from a Woody Allen movie," says Danny. "'You know we're going to have this kiss eventually, so we may as well have it right now.'" The date went until 5 a.m., concluding with him asking to listen to tapes of Audrey's singing; "I really knew he liked me then," says Audrey, laughing. He left and when she woke up the next day, there was a note under her door from Danny saying he'd had a good time. "So we were in love," says Audrey.

She took her first trip to Europe that fall, celebrating her 26th birthday with him in Paris. When he moved back, they started dating seriously, but they were both wary of marriage.

"Both of us come from divorced families," says Audrey. Her parents divorced after 33 years together, and Danny's divorced after 25 years. "We both witnessed really bad marriages and we were a little gun-shy."

They decided to ease into commitment by living together. "We wanted to make sure it was right," says Danny. They were both at the outset of developing their careers—Audrey working in magazine ad sales at Condé Nast, and Danny opening his first restaurant, Union Square Cafe, in 1985.

While moving in together is a serious step for any couple, getting engaged is a formality that is as much a promise to one another as it is to friends and family. It allows other people to share in and celebrate a couple's commitment. After two years of living together, in June 1987, they received terrible family news: Audrey's mother was diagnosed with lung cancer and told she had six months to live. "I was devastated, because my mom was going to die and she wouldn't get to see us married," says Audrey.

That October, Danny proposed. "I wanted to be able to tell Audrey's mom about the engagement," says Danny. They married in August 1988; they were both 30.

Danny chose to open six of his restaurants in Union Square to take advantage of the Greenmarket there, and he and Audrey live in the same area. Modern art pieces are hung alongside family photos over the fireplaces in their elegant, high-ceiling apartment overlooking Gramercy Park.

Not everything is perfect inside on this September afternoon. The majority of their carpets are missing, sent off to the cleaner due to the arrival of a new puppy (now being trained). A mix-up with the math tutor has Audrey on her iPhone with the orthodontist trying to rearrange one of their children's schedules. Meanwhile, Danny is trying to get ahold of their daughter via text message. Amid the hubbub, they continue to entertain their guests, while laughing at the inconveniences—this is a couple well-trained in hospitality.

Over the two decades of their marriage, Danny's career has thrived; he has opened more than 10 restaurants—all found on "Best of" lists in New York—and written a book, *Setting the Table: The Power of Hospitality in Restaurants, Business, and Life*.

"What I've tried to do through these years is just to let Danny go, and let him pursue what he wants to pursue, and travel where he needs to travel to follow his dream," says Audrey, who has focused on raising their four children. "I never wanted to be in a relationship where I was holding someone back from doing that, so that's been part of my commitment—to support him in that."

Danny confers with Audrey on major decisions about the company and restaurant sites. And he is now supporting her as she has started again pursuing singing and acting opportunities, and performing in operas and musicals.

"Commitment means being there for the other person. We've had some ups and downs in our lives," says Audrey. Between the birth of their first child and that of their twins, Audrey had a first set of twins who were born prematurely and did not survive. That loss still brings tears to Audrey's eyes, but the emotional trauma brought them closer. "We were able to stick together through a sad, awful time. It was a real strain on our relationship for a while. It was very painful, but it made us so much stronger. I know that sounds cliché. But once you've seen the dark hole of something like that, and can recover from it, it builds such a glue."

Danny squeezes her hand and looks at her with his blue eyes, striking in a deeply tanned face. " We remain on one another's side through thick and thin. You can't be a fair-weather friend," he says. They heard a statistic at the time—a statistic now questioned in academic circles—that the vast preponderance of marriages don't survive the loss of a child. "We thought, 'We'll be damned if we're part of that statistic,'" says Danny. "It was the same attitude we had before getting married."

Years back, Pesca closed and the space was taken over by Bobby Flay's Bolo. Flay knew the Meyers had met there and called them in 2007 to let them know the building was being torn down. He invited them for the restaurant's last night on New Year's Eve. The stairway may now be gone, but the "glance" lives on. "Out of the blue, you're looking at each other and just get that flush," says Audrey.

And they've memorialized their first meeting in another way. They founded a charity with an inheritance from Danny's grandfather, to give grants to community organizations that support food hunger relief, parks and classic theater. They named it the Stairway Foundation. ❋

Pam & George Friedman | Second Chances

WHEN PAM FIRST MET GEORGE, she "couldn't stand him." A friend threw a dinner party in January 1990 and had sat the two divorcées next to one another hoping they would hit off. They had discussed books, and Pam was frustrated that George kept interrupting her. She thought he wasn't listening to her.

George had a different reaction. He was listening and was interrupting because he was so excited to be talking to her. "There was chemistry the moment I met her," he says. "Pam has a warm, strong personality and she takes over a room. I was immediately attracted to her."

Despite her initial dislike, Pam had a messenger deliver a book to George the next day. "He was a voracious reader and I was a literary agent," says Pam. She sent a biography she had mentioned to him, of Judah P. Benjamin, the "Henry Kissinger of the Confederacy."

George is an entrepreneur who has started and sold a number of toiletry and fragrance companies, including a fragrances joint venture with Ralph Lauren and the development of a toiletries line with The Limited for Bath and Body Works and Victoria's Secret. He has taught at Columbia and M.I.T. Business Schools, namely a class called "Intuition as a Key Element of Success." It's safe to say that his intuition when it came to Pam was that she would be a good match for him. When the book arrived, George got Pam's number from the accompanying William Morris letterhead, where Pam was then a vice-president. He called to thank her for the book and to ask her out on a date.

Pam's young assistants often asked her for romantic advice and she always told them to give someone a second chance. Having been single for 15 years, after divorcing her first husband, she decided to take her own advice. She and George went out the following Friday and had a much better time.

"I may have been intimidated the first time I met him," says Pam. "Or maybe George was just too perfect."

"I knew by the second or third date that this was it," says George. "We had so much to talk about it." He knew it was right, because on several trips out to the Hamptons, they would be so engrossed in conversation that he would miss his the turn-off on the highway. In 25 years of making that commute, he had never done that before.

"For me, I never asked anybody for help. I was very independent," says Pam, who was 44 when they met. One of her sons had a fantasy of working on a boat in Australia and she found herself asking George for advice about it. "That surprised me. I never consulted other people before."

They got married eight months later, in September 1990, purchasing a new apartment so that there would be room for their combined families. Between the two of them, they suddenly had three nineteen-year-old boys—George's son and Pam's twins. The families merged happily. "George wasn't just marrying me. He was marrying my family," says Pam.

Sitting on opposite sides of the couch in the library of their Park Avenue apartment, Pam tends to dominate the conversation, while George gives her free rein, looking on amused. Behind them, on the wall, a snake watches as a naked Adam waves off an apple offered by Eve.

"Since we'd both been divorced, we understand how easy it is to walk away from something," says Pam. "But in the long run, if it's the right person, it's so much more rewarding to work through it and get to the next level of the relationship."

Problems ultimately strengthen the commitment, if you make it through them. "You need to go through a lot of bumps and come out on the other side," adds George. "It either falls apart, or it gets stronger and the commitment gets deeper."

That's what happened for these two. They are a couple that thrives on their differences. "In the beginning, you think of the differences as threatening," says Pam.

"I'm linear and logical and she's warm and emotional," adds George. "My weakness fits with her strength and vice versa. And we've learned over the years how to make our two personalities mesh better."

"Over time, you realize you respect the differences," says Pam. "He shows me a new way of looking at something and I can learn from that."

Looking back on their first marriages, Pam and George think they were too unformed to choose the right partner. "When you're young, you may not know yourself well enough to know what you really need," says George.

"I don't think you can really understand commitment when you're younger. You think you do, but life does strange things, and you have to be strong enough to be able to handle those things. And that takes a certain maturity—a maturity that I certainly didn't have when I got married at 23," says Pam. "You can work really hard at something, but if it's not meant to be, it will not be."

When it is meant to be, it is a rich and fulfilling part of life. "Through the good times and the bad times, you are there for the other person, 100 percent. And it's not a burden. It's a pleasure," says Pam. ※

Ed & Magda Bleier | I and Thou

ED BLEIER'S MEETING MAGDA was the result of a karmic debt owed to him by his best friend, Bill Safire, the legendary *New York Times* columnist.

Magda, a French journalist, was seated beside Safire at a dinner party in Paris. Safire found her to be utterly delightful. Years earlier, Ed had met a "gorgeous" British woman— a sister of a woman he was then dating—and suggested that Safire meet her. Theirs was a whirlwind romance, and within weeks, they were married. After their wedding in 1962, Safire presented Ed with a silver matchbox engraved, "To Ed, the perfect matchmaker— from one of his matches."

After the Parisian dinner party in 1972, Safire gave his friend a better gift. Magda had told him over dinner that she planned to travel to the States to conduct interviews. Safire gave her Ed's number and told Ed, "I met this charming French journalist and she's going to call you."

Ed was in his early 40s by that time, a successful motion picture executive at Warner Bros., and a very satisfied and active New York City bachelor. Then he met Magda; he realized within a year that she was worth giving up his bachelor lifestyle.

Ed and Magda both had input from friends early in their relationship. Ed especially needed a push to give up the single life he had led for decades.

He lived in a top-floor Fifth Avenue apartment next to the Guggenheim. "I lived there because I wanted a Frank Lloyd Wright sculpture in my living room," he says. A friend lived in an apartment below his. When Ed left the building with dates, the neighbor would surreptitiously give him a thumbs up or a thumbs down. When the neighbor met Magda, he called Ed and said, "Our friendship is over if you don't marry that woman."

Magda, then in her twenties and in the flush of her journalistic career, was debating whether to return to Europe or to stay in the U.S. to be with Ed. A French friend asked her three defining questions:

"Do you like his 'skin?'"—meaning his physical attractiveness and presence.

"Do you want to have children with him?"

"Imagine your last moment in life… Whose hand do you want in your hand?"

Her answers were "yes" to the first two and "Ed" for the last, so she knew he was the one. "Maybe these questions seem simplistic," says Magda, in French-accented English. "But they are profound at the same time."

Of course, Magda only wanted to stay if Ed felt a similar level of commitment. "Having not married until then, I had some anxiety about marriage," says Ed. "Magda said to me, 'What is our future? You're the only reason I'm staying here.' Suddenly I was more worried about losing her than committing to her." They married in 1973.

Talking about their commitment seems to come easily to the Bleiers. Magda says: "The word *commitment* has a connotation of obligation. I feel no obligation. I wanted a man I loved, respected, trusted and admired. I found all of this in Ed. It just seemed natural that we would be together. For me, loving one another is instinctive and natural."

"Commitment means the relationship has to be the priority," she adds. "Always be there for one another."

Magda says honesty and open communication are keys to their partnership. "I like mystery, but I don't like secrecy," she says, and quotes the French author André Maurois. "A happy marriage is a long conversation which always seems too short."

Ed says: "My view of commitment is mutual respect—for the differences as well as the similarities. Though it's very difficult, it's often the accommodation of the differences that's most important. Not trying to merge but to be mutually interdependent."

Ed references an Austrian philosopher to help explain his meaning of commitment. "I keep recalling an aphorism of Martin Buber, a philosopher who talked about 'I-Thou,'" says Ed, citing "Ich-Du," Buber's work on how humans actualize their existence. "The feelings of self are so profoundly improved by the ability to have a commitment to someone else that you not only love the somebody else but you like yourself even more because you're able to give the love."

Ed and Magda are able to intellectualize their commitment, but there's also a sheer joy and positive energy that emanates from them when they are together. "A human being is an energy machine," says Ed. "Best that the energy goes into work and love."

For this reason, Ed stays busy with corporate and pro bono boards. Additionally, in 2003, he published a best-selling book, *The Thanksgiving Ceremony*, and is now writing a professional book.

They have no children of their own, but Magda's family is extensive. Ed and Magda are very close to her nieces, nephews (and godsons), one of whom lived with them for two and a half years after he graduated from Syracuse University (which Ed also attended, and where he was a classmate with Safire). "These are terrific relationships: all the joy of off-spring and none of the difficulties," says Ed.

Ed and Magda relate strongly to one another and consider theirs a great partnership. Their palpable joie de vivre together makes it clear why commitment comes so naturally to them. ※

Howard & Ellen Greenberg
Knowing What You Want

UPON FIRST MEETING HOWARD AND ELLEN, it's immediately obvious how they balance one another. Howard is calm and steady, while the vibrant Ellen is full of hyperkinetic energy, whirling about him like the wind around a tall, leafy oak tree.

Ellen's golden-brown wavy hair is thick and wild on this rainy March night, her light, green eyes set off by a ruddy complexion that seems undaunted by months of winter. "I love the winter," she says. "I'm an outdoorsy person, and love skiing."

Howard does not. They're currently closing on a condo in Miami so as to have an escape from it. "I don't like Florida, but Howard hates the winter," Ellen says. "Commitment is compromise: balancing what you want with what they want."

Howard has wanted a place in Florida for years, and Ellen finally gave in after a particularly, brutal winter in New York. "Will I like Miami?" she asks rhetorically. "Probably not, but I'll tolerate it for him."

Howard has just come from his photography gallery in Manhattan's midtown. He wears a pale green sweater over a blue-collared shirt, while Ellen is dressed more casually in a black peasant shirt paired with a brown polka-dotted scarf.

Howard says the two made a deal when they got married. "I would take care of business and finance and she would take care of home and kids," he says. "And she is amazing at that."

They met in Woodstock, New York, in the late 1980s. "We shared lots of interests," says Ellen. "Except golf."

Howard had been married before to "an ambitious woman." They had started a business, but it had never been a priority to start a family together—something for which they were both thankful when they divorced. "I wasn't looking to get married again so fast but I really wanted a family," says Howard. When he met Ellen, she made it clear that her

priority was to be a mother. "I'm a traditional, old-fashioned girl," she says. "I never knew what I wanted to do. I just wanted children."

They married in September 1988 when Ellen was 31, and Howard was 40. It rained on their wedding day, leading someone to tell Ellen it was a good sign, meaning she was very fertile. That person was right. Ellen and Howard had their first daughter within a year. Twins came three years later.

"For all her insanity and craziness, Ellen would step in front of a car for her children—and probably for me," says Howard. "She has an incredibly strong maternal instinct. I felt that from the beginning and it was important to me."

Meanwhile, Howard focused his energies on building his gallery. When he and Ellen first moved to Manhattan, there were fewer than 10 photography galleries in the city. It was a new concept at the time.

Howard had previously been a newspaper photographer in Woodstock, making very little money—about $50 per week, and another $67 per week working part time in a post office. He was also an amateur "treasure hunter," searching for rarities in upstate New York's yard sales and antique shops. When he purchased a collection of photography journals from the turn of the century—*Camera Notes*, edited by the renowned photographer Alfred Steiglitz—for $1,100, he knew he had discovered something very valuable.

"I read them cover to cover. It changed my life," he says. "I knew they were too valuable for me to hang on to, though."

He sold them for $17,000. "I considered it Steiglitz blood money," he says. He used part of the profits to start a photography center in Woodstock. "The rest of my career grew from there," says Howard, who is now one of the top photography dealers in the country.

The gallery's initial, fevered growth coincided with his daughters' births and childhood. It took many years before he could give up working on Saturdays, which was tough for Ellen. "Commitment is being there for your partner during the highs and lows, good times and bad times," she says.

"It's how strong you are during the most trying times," says Howard, while sipping a green tea. "It's very easy to throw in the towel. For every couple, there are difficult moments. Commitment is figuring out how to get through them and how to renew yourselves from them."

Ellen laments that people give up on relationships too easily. While no one should stay married if they're unhappy, she says, there's something wonderful about being with someone for a long time. "You have a history and memories together. You get to share the happy times—like your children's graduations—and support each other through the difficult times, such as family members' deaths, Howard's back and knee surgeries, and our daughter's spinal fusion operation," she says. "Now I look forward to the future we'll share—being grandparents and having a big family."

There is much joy from the life that they share together, but their commitment also demands sacrifices. "It requires selflessness at times," says Howard. "You want something for yourself, but you have to give it up, and you have to try to do that with grace."

Howard attributes his current understanding of commitment to a weekend-long seminar he did in the early 1980s before meeting Ellen. It was an est training led by Werner Erhard, whose personal transformation seminars—which had originated in federal prisons in the late 1970s—were a popular trend then, attracting celebrities like Cher, Diana Ross, Yoko Ono and Jeff Bridges.

"A lot of it was hokey, but there were some important lessons. The primary thing for me was the concept of responsibility. No one does it to you; you do it. You create your life. At the end of the day, all you have is your word and that's commitment," says Howard. "If you say you're going to do something, you commit to it. From being on time to returning phone calls—you make these promises to other people. It's the same with Ellen with our wedding vows."

Being able to look into Ellen's eyes every day and know that he's honored his vows brings him great satisfaction. Ellen laughs, summing things up with a joke. "I'm very committed to Howard, and he's very committed to golf." ※

Lester & Geri Pollack | The Vows Say It All

THESE TWO BROOKLYN NATIVES met as summer camp counselors in upstate New York in 1952. Their feelings for one another developed during days off spent boating or swimming or hitching rides into town to see movies.

It wasn't just a summer romance. They kept dating when they went back to college, and got engaged a few years later. Lester, then a loan-strapped law student, couldn't afford an engagement ring when he first proposed. He decided to spend a summer working in Atlantic City in order to raise money for the ring. He was turned down for a waiter's job at a Loews hotel, but managed to find employment at a "Boardwalk Frankfurt estate," he says. (In other words, a hotdog stand.) He saved up the money needed, and they married after Geri graduated from college and after Lester's second year at New York University Law School.

Geri has auburn hair and delicate features. She waits patiently and lovingly as Lester speaks. Once a talented public orator, he speaks more slowly these days as he meets the challenges of Parkinson's disease. Dressed in a black suit with gold cufflinks and a yellow tie, he defines commitment in very formal terms. "Our values and course of conduct reflect that we're binding to each other to assure the best happens in building a marriage and a relationship," says Lester. "It's a sense of support in trying new things to advance the quality of life and the joy of the partnership."

These two have built a very wonderful life together, taking great joy in their children, grandchildren, and their philanthropy, even though they started with very little. Their first home together was a small apartment in Sheepshead Bay, Brooklyn. Those were less comfortable times. In the winter, for example, there was no heat, as their landlord didn't provide it. "We would put the kids in the crib in their snowsuits at night," says Geri.

After graduating from law school, though, Lester's career ascended rapidly. "Lester was the business person and I was the at-home person, particularly in the first half of our marriage," says Geri. Lester started out at a corporate law firm and then took a position at Loews Corporation as its legal counsel. A public company owned by the Tisch family, Larry and Bob Tisch asked Lester to meet with their mother, Sadie, before hiring him. When he was introduced, he told her about the summer in Atlantic City when he was turned down by a Loews hotel for a waiter job. "Well," Sadie Tisch replied. "We were saving you for the big one."

That was the first step on a path that led Lester away from law and into business and finance. He became involved in the company's mergers and acquisitions, and learned about the world of investment. He was eventually made Loews Corporation's executive vice president, and then left to become a founding partner at an investment firm. He eventually founded the private equity firm Centre Partners, where he remains a managing director.

Now Lester and Geri live in a high-ceilinged Fifth Avenue home in Manhattan that seems to float above Central Park, cloud-like with its beige-toned art collection, ivory walls, and cream-colored couch. A white orchid rests delicately upon a table, a reminder of the inherent beauty of fragile objects.

They are both hyper aware of the power of education to transform a person's circumstances, and so have given back to New York University Law School over the years. Lester was the chairman of the law school board for over a decade, and committed himself to helping to transform it into one of the country's top schools. He also chaired the Conference of Presidents of Major American Jewish Organizations. Meanwhile, as a first-generation American, Geri focuses her energies primarily on philanthropy involving community organizations that help acculturate immigrants to the U.S.

"We started off with very little, so giving back is important to us," Geri says. "I think it's very fortunate we started off that way and got to build our life together. We have a great appreciation of our success and a great desire to give back."

Now in their 70s, Lester and Geri are encouraging their two children and grandchildren to feel similarly responsible to those less fortunate than they are. Their commitment to one another is not insular; instead it blossoms as a mutual desire to improve upon the world around them. The strength of their relationship buttresses those efforts, whether it's contributing toward museums or helping to shape foreign policy through community organizations.

And their strong relationship provides a solid firmament for when they do face hardships. "Commitment in our marriage was set in our vows—to love, honor, and protect each other throughout our lives together," says Geri. In sickness and in health, for richer or for poorer, these two are bound to each other and happily so. ※

Antonio & Rosa De Mitri | Grande Amore

WHEN ASKED WHAT HELPED make their fifty-year marriage work, Rosa and Antonio both say, "Gelosia."

"Jealousy," translates their youngest son, Roberto, who acted as interpreter for their interview, and who has been together in a relationship for ten years with Elizabeth Hamburg, the daughter of Morton I. Hamburg, the photographer, and who is learning the meaning of commitment.

Rosa, dressed in black with her red hair swept back in pins, smiles as she recalls the dramatic lengths to which her husband went to reassure himself about their commitment. They met in 1955 in Lecce—a historic city at the bottom of the stiletto of the boot-shaped Italy. Antonio, then 20, was part of the Carabinieri—Italy's military police force—and was home for just a few days.

After two meetings, it became a "grande amore," says Rosa, who was then 17. She asked Antonio to meet her family immediately, because at that time in Italy, two young people couldn't see each other unless the family agreed to it. Even after getting the family's approval and becoming engaged, they couldn't go out and walk around town without a family member chaperoning.

There were other romantic restrictions beyond the familial ones. As a member of the Carabinieri, Antonio could not get married until age 28. So their engagement was a long one: eight years. (Roberto jokes to his fiancée, "Long engagements run in the family.")

Antonio says that it was very difficult for him to live in a different town from Rosa during the engagement; he wrote daily letters to her and would "surprise" visit her every two weeks. Rosa's uncle suggested she buy a present for the postman who had to deliver Antonio's constant flow of love letters.

They finally married in 1962 and moved to Rome and then to Milan. Antonio was

chief of the Carabinieri station for the Italian Air Force. Though Rosa was a skilled seamstress, she did not work outside of the home. Due to his jealousy, Antonio wanted her to always be at home in case he wanted to surprise her. He also thought this accorded better with the strict moral conduct expected of the wife of a Carabinieri chief in a highly patriarchal society. Rosa did not mind being confined to the home—she was in love, and enjoyed being taken care of.

Antonio's jealousy seems almost theatrical. They would go dancing every Saturday night, and Antonio would dance to every song, because he did not want Rosa to be asked by anyone else. Early in their marriage, Antonio wrote a letter to Rosa pretending to be a stranger courting her. He wanted to see if she would leave the house to meet this stranger. She passed his test, but he remained jealous.

Rosa complained about his jealousy, but accepted it. They say that the constant tension strengthened the relationship, keeping it passionate. It also helped fuel a mutual life-long love of dancing. They've participated in and won many ballroom dancing competitions over the years.

When they had children, Rosa became the jealous one. She was utterly focused on her three children and paid them the kind of close attention that Antonio had lavished on her.

One thing that helped make their partnership work was their complementary manners—Antonio's passion was balanced with Rosa's level-headedness. While he is an avowed romantic, she admits she's not, describing herself as "cold." Antonio was actually reassured by this, as it made him more certain that she would not be stolen away by some other man's grand romantic gestures. Meanwhile, Rosa took her husband's ferventness in stride and was never flustered by it.

Antonio eventually left the Carabinieri to work as head of security for a private energy company in 1980. Rosa remained at home. Their traditional roles did not change dramatically until 2004, when Antonio developed throat cancer.

Antonio had to have an operation to have his larynx removed and today speaks with a mechanical larynx. He spent a year recovering, and was very depressed about losing his voice. They say this made them closer. Rosa never made Antonio feel like a burden, even in his darkest moments. She accepted his sickness and his new restrictions, and took care of him. Meanwhile, he became less demanding, encouraging her to go out of the house more and spend time with her friends.

After a year, they were invited to be in a big dance competition in Southern Italy. There, Antonio felt free of his cancer; no one knew his voice was gone as they floated around the dance floor. And Rosa's eyes were only on him, as they've always been.

Jealousy aside, they say there's no secret to why their relationship works. "It's just a day-to-day proposition," says Antonio. "You're thankful for every day you have together and you enjoy it." ✻

Susan Calhoun & Charlie Moss
From Fearing to Freeing

SUSAN AND CHARLIE MAKE A STRIKING COUPLE. They both wear their silver hair long—Charlie's wavy mane falling a few inches below his ears and Susan's like a white-silver waterfall cascading down her back. Charlie's eyes are brown, warm, and reassuring, while Susan's are bright, blue, and flashing.

They live in an ornate apartment on Fifth Avenue looking onto Central Park. "Come in, come in. Would you like something to drink?" says Susan. "I need coffee, strong coffee," she adds, though she barely seems to need it. Susan's mercurial energy makes it difficult for her to keep her seat for very long.

The phone rings and she jumps up to get it. When she returns, she springs up again—"I'm thinking if it's cold for the wedding weekend, perhaps I should wear this," she says to Charlie as she models a dark green velvet shawl, which makes her large blue eyes and long silver hair even more striking.

She sits down but then glances out the window and spots a commotion in front of the building. "Look at this, the police are here." She bounces up again to put in a call to the doorman to find out what's going on.

Meanwhile, Charlie launches into the story of how they met, and it becomes clear that settling down has long been a challenge for Susan.

It was 1974. Charlie, 37, was a divorced bachelor working as a partner in an advertising agency. While lunching with a disgruntled employee at the Plaza Hotel Oyster Bar, he saw a "vision of a beautiful girl." Susan, a television commercial producer, was talking to an advertising director with whom Charlie was acquainted, so he went over and introduced himself.

He went back to work and called her immediately to ask her to dinner with friends the next night. She said she was busy, and Charlie told her she should break the date. She did. "We all went to El Morocco. Susan and I spent the night drinking and dancing and smooching," says Charlie, who was immediately smitten and invited her to go to an advertising convention with him that weekend and stay in his suite. She refused.

"All weekend, I'm calling her, sending her flowers, telling everyone at the convention I've met the girl I'm going to marry," says Charlie.

Susan has returned from her police investigation, and Charlie gets her to settle into a chair. "Do you want to pick it up?" he asks.

"I told my roommate he was crazy," says Susan. "But he was persistent."

"She was elusive," says Charlie. "She was impossible. The things I did in order to keep her on the hook, so to speak, were monumental. It was a tremendous amount of energy and creativity. Poems and songs and flowers."

"I asked her to marry me on our second date. She said no," Charlie continues. "And I kept asking her for the next two years and she kept saying no."

It seems fair to say that Susan was a commitment-phobe. She enjoyed her independence and, by age 32, had grown overly accustomed to being single. But Charlie's persistence helped bring on an epiphany.

"I remember walking down Park Avenue and feeling really dizzy, and absolutely realizing that unless I did something different than what I was doing, I was never going to be married," said Susan. "It wasn't that I didn't want to be married. It was just that I was so nervous about it that I was putting it off."

She finally relented and moved in with Charlie in 1976, but she was still reluctant to get married. Part of the reason for that was that she wanted to have children and Charlie, who already had a son from his first marriage, did not.

They argued about this for months but could not come to a resolution. One afternoon, Susan was on the phone talking about the problem with her mother when an actress came in who would be interviewing for a commercial. The actress overheard the discussion and offered this advice: "Just on the other side of no is yes."

Susan met Charlie after the interview and spent the whole lunch talking about why they should have children. He did not say a word, but then walked her back to her office and as he dropped her off, said: "Will you marry me, kids and all?"

"I helped that actress get lots of commercials," adds Susan. She and Charlie married in 1977.

Not surprisingly, Susan thinks of commitment as something that's still changing and evolving. "The living part of a commitment is what's really interesting. It's not that you stay committed, it's that you shift around in the commitment," she says. "It's very alive—that's the good in it. If it's not alive, that's when there's problems."

Charlie thinks of it more mechanically, with moving parts that one comes to understand over time. "When I first got married to Susan, I wasn't thinking about specifics, I was thinking about the general feeling of being in love and the future with her in a very abstract way," says Charlie, reflecting on how his understanding of commitment has changed over the decades. "As you progress down the path, things come up—problems and obstacles. Things which you either work together to solve or you don't. And if you work together to solve them, you get a stronger sense of what the commitment is. That's the difference between today and 30 years ago. Now I'm more aware of what those problems might be and more aware of our strengths to solve those problems. We have a really strong mechanism that allows us to work through differences even when we're totally opposed on an issue."

The issue of children continued to be an obstacle for them. They tried to get pregnant for seven years, with Susan having two operations, Charlie having one, and their enrolling in an in vitro program in its early days at Columbia Hospital. When Susan was ovulating, Charlie would go to great lengths to see her, such as the time when she was in California working on a commercial. "I had to hop on a plane and head out there so I could service her," he says.

And when Susan was menstruating, it was devastating. "I would call Charlie and say, 'Scarlet came.' He would then leave his meeting or wherever he was and talk to me. I would be weeping or angry," she says. "I could always count on him to let me be sad for a few minutes on the phone. There were no cell phones than, and I remember looking for a pay phone sometimes, and just needing to sit in that phone booth and be upset."

After Susan turned 40, they decided to adopt instead, welcoming two Korean children into their family. They now find humor in their infertility struggles and use the tales of mushed Fallopian tubes and hospital-mandated masturbation as fodder for the Narativ Storytelling Workshop—you can find them on YouTube. "It's like going through a war and you've been in a battle and you've survived," says Charlie. "We're on the other end of it. At the time it wasn't so funny. It was death-defying, but now it's amusing."

"Struggles are what make you grow and become more aware of who you are. It's not necessarily the good times or the best times that make your commitment stronger," says Susan. "You have to look at the horror as an opportunity."

Susan, who was terrified in her 30s of being trapped, now thinks of commitment as "freeing." She uses an analogy of a city to describe it. "If you visit a city and you have two weeks, you only do certain things in that city," she says, drawing a parallel to the variety but limited opportunities of non-committed relationships. "If you're going to a city to live, though, you get to do different things and explore it more fully. It's a whole different way of being. It's very freeing if it's the right person." ※

Mandy Patinkin & Kathryn Grody | Cliff Jumpers

ON A SUNDAY NIGHT IN JANUARY, Kathryn sits on the couch with one leg curled under her, while Mandy lounges in a recliner, his leg thrown over the armrest. The voice of their youngest son, Gideon, 24, booms through their Upper West Side apartment as he runs through singing exercises in a back room.

Theirs is a family of performers. Mandy—an actor and singer whose favorite on-screen role was the revenge-seeking Inigo Montoya in Rob Reiner's *The Princess Bride*—and Kathryn—a stage actress—recount their romantic history dramatically, describing scenes vividly and using voices to capture characters they met along the way.

"She robbed the cradle," says Mandy, now 58. When they first met, cast together at Manhattan's Ensemble Studio Theater in 1978, he was 25 and Kathryn was 31. Mandy was the male lead in a Michael Weller play called *The Split*, about a couple that had just broken up. Kathryn played a mutual friend of the couple.

They had one scene together. Over dinner at an Italian restaurant with red-and-white checkered tablecloths, Kathryn was supposed to console Mandy's character, while he tried his best to seduce her.

"During our first rehearsal, we began to improvise, saying all the things that people say to each other when they first meet, the games they play," says Mandy. "We were like jazz musicians, going back and forth, just making great music."

The interplay between them grew so intense that their director felt excluded and left them to it. "It was like six weeks of courting condensed into a 45-minute improvisation," says Mandy.

They did not date during the play's short two-month run, though. Both had rules against courting co-workers. Moreover, Kathryn had a rule against dating her own kind. "The only thing I knew when I left college was that I was never going to marry and that I wouldn't date an actor," she says. "Because I knew I was going to have a life in the theater and that one in the family of theatricals is enough."

Of course, post-collegial certainties about how we will live our lives do not always come to fruition, and Mandy would overturn Kathryn's convictions on both counts. The play finished on a Saturday night, and Mandy presented Kathryn with a wrapped gift. She felt the present was soft, so she didn't open it in front of him. "The kid has given me something to wear," she worried. She did read the card, though. Mandy had written, "With my love, my hopes, my dreams, my fears, the future."

When she got home that night at 2 a.m., she opened the present, and immediately called Mandy. "I loved the shawl and I liked the blouse," she told him.

Gideon walks into the room at this point in the storytelling and recites Mandy's response in concert with his mother: "You hated the blouse, huh? I wasn't sure about the blouse. I never bought clothes for a woman before." The story has been mythologized in the family, and told often to their two sons.

They spent hours on the phone. Kathryn read him lots of angry feminist poetry. Mandy searched his apartment for a book of poems to respond in kind. In a friend's collection, he found the poem "The Country of Marriage" and read that to Kathryn. "I grabbed it because I wanted her to like me," says Mandy. "'I give you my death to set you free of me' was a line from it, and I loved it."

"It's a miracle that we got past my angry feminism poetry," says Kathryn. "The-25-year-old's poem was profound—and has longevity and legs. We now reread it every year on the anniversary of our first April date."

"You don't need a lot of books of poetry. You just need to find the one right poem," says Mandy.

The next day they went to brunch in Greenwich Village. He arrived with a bouquet of yellow mums. "I just have one thing to say before brunch," he told her. "I'm going to marry you." She responded, "Well, you're going to get very hurt. I'm not going to marry anyone. I don't believe in it."

Kathryn was deeply rooted in feminist thought and saw marriage as a subjugation of the female to the male. "Mandy missed the 60s and I was formed by them," she says. Mandy said he'd be patient.

After brunch, they had their first kiss on a corner outside of the restaurant, right by a

garbage can. "Love. Isn't it wonderful?" said an elderly African-American man in a deep, beautiful voice as he walked by. Mandy responded, "Yes, it is."

A year later, they got engaged, and in 1980, they married. They inscribed the phrase "In loving trust" on the insides of their wedding bands. "I don't need people to get married to be a couple," says Mandy. "But I do need there to be some sort of spiritual or religious marker."

Mandy wanted a proper Jewish wedding, even though he did not consider himself particularly religious. "I wanted a religious ceremony because spiritual ceremonies are beyond what I know and understand. They are more powerful than what I can get a grasp of," he says. "And what I was feeling, and have continued to feel for 32 years—which some people use the word *love* for—has always been more than what I can understand."

Mandy cites Shakespeare to explain: "Hamlet says to Horatio, 'There are more things in heaven and earth than are dreamt of in your philosophy. Therefore, as a stranger, give it welcome.'"

And how did Kathryn let go of her feminist opposition to marriage?

"All those academic, intellectual, and theoretical ideas fell away versus the practice. It bothered me that people would say, 'Oh, you're just living together,'" says Kathryn. "All these ideas you have about yourself and who you're going to be were coming up against who I was discovering I really was. I did not know of another public way beyond marriage to say this person is different from all the other people I've loved."

During their engagement, Kathryn went to see Mandy performing in *Evita* on Broadway. She was sitting behind Henry Fonda. "This Patinkin kid. This can't be his first musical," Fonda remarked to his wife during an intermission.

"Yes, it is actually," Kathryn interrupted.

"Oh, are you related to him?" Fonda replied.

"Well, I'm about to be," she said, and it was very meaningful to her to be able to say that. Marriage would establish them as two people officially related to one another.

"Suddenly, all my theory about why marriage was a bad institution for women—how it had to do with ownership and men owning woman—the history of it was very irrelevant to how I felt about this person," says Kathryn. "I wanted this person to be the father of my children. All my theory fell away in the truer emotional need I had to be connected to Mandy."

Now married 30 years, Mandy thinks back fondly on their first kiss. "It's significant to me that the old man on the corner spoke to us on the sidewalk by the garbage can," he says. "I think that garbage can being there was quite profound, because a life is filled with wonderful things and garbage. And that old man focused on the kiss and the love and not the garbage."

There have been hard times. Mandy and Kathryn had two periods of separation in their marriage—for six months and for eight months. Mandy attributes it to his mid-life crisis at 50. They were arguing frequently. "It was killing me to create pain for someone I loved so dearly," says Mandy, so they separated.

But while apart, they missed each other profoundly and realized they couldn't live without the other. When the troubles were over, Kathryn gave Mandy a new thin silver wedding ring with two bumps—one big and one little that signified their periods of separation. The ring had new texture, but "it was still complete," says Kathryn.

"The assumption that marriage means you're going to last forever and that's what the commitment is is wrong," says Kathryn. "That's what always terrified me about marriage: the idea of settling down, of becoming one, and then becoming something static and unchanging. In fact, you keep evolving who you are. After 30 years, I think commitment is re-choosing on a continual basis to re-embrace aspects of this person."

When they got engaged in 1979 and went to speak to their rabbi, he noted Kathryn's continuing discomfort with the idea of marriage and told them that he thought their union was a "real leap of faith." Kathryn still thinks of their relationship that way.

"For me, it means we keep leaping. You think you just come to one cliff and you grab hands and leap," says Kathryn. "But in a long relationship, you keep coming to new and different cliffs, and you keep making the decision to go together and see if you land." ※

John R. & Wendy Gambling | Realistic Expectations

FOR CITIZENS OF THE EMPIRE STATE, John's name and voice are recognizable ones. He is the third in a line of John Gamblings who have hosted a New York morning radio show since 1925. Every Friday on WOR, Mayor Michael Bloomberg joins John to talk about current issues in the city.

But when Wendy first met John in 1975, she had no idea who he was, since she had grown up in South Jersey. Wendy, then 22, had just finished college and was staying with her sister and brother-in-law in Plantation, Florida. John, then 24, was in a neighboring townhouse, while working as a program director at WAXY radio station in Fort Lauderdale. They met in a Publix parking lot.

"Wendy was on a bicycle eating ice cream with her sister," says John. Wendy's sister introduced the two of them as John was loading groceries into his car. John soon went to Wendy's brother-in-law to ask whether he could take her out on a date. Being from Westchester, New York, Wendy's brother-in-law was very impressed when he found out John's full name. Wendy, on the other hand, was mildly inconvenienced by it. Her maiden name is Gamberling, and the postman had been dropping her mail in John's box all summer.

Theirs was an unusual first date. "It was a promotional event at the radio station—'Bachelors 3' with [then New York Jets quarterback] Joe Namath. Blood, Sweat, & Tears were playing. So I asked Wendy to join me for some blood, sweat, and tears," says John. "The rest is history. It didn't take very long."

They married in June 1976 at the Hotel du Pont in Wilmington, Delaware. They now live in Long Island, but on this February evening are preparing to depart for the warmer climes of their house on Florida's west coast.

"I don't think there's anything more important than commitment," says John. "For a lot of people, it's a very hard thing to do. For me, it's not hard at all, because it truly is the centerpiece of life. There's no other way to move in any direction unless you are committed to something or, in this case, to someone. There's no way to create a family or synergy of friends if you don't have a commitment to someone, or something or some ones. It comes in commitment to job, church, community service, whatever it is. If you don't care about anything or anyone else, how can you care about yourself?"

For John, the word *commitment* has purely positive connotations. He does not think of it as a burden but as the necessary foundation upon which to build the entirety of his life.

"The only way you can identify yourself is through others, and how you give to them, and hopefully, how they give back to you," he says.

Wendy is more light-hearted in her description of their commitment. "We've stuck it out through the good and some of the bad. We're raised three fabulous sons together. I'm so committed I've yet to put a pillow over his head because his snoring is so awful," she says, laughing. "I can only hope and pray that the next 35 years will be just as great."

For their 35th anniversary this summer, they're planning to do a cruise on the Dalmation coast line and go to Croatia. "We're working on that right now. Hopefully, it happens," says Wendy. It sounds like a fairy-tale anniversary, but John warns against fairy tales.

"Because of modern culture, films and TV shows, people expect too much. They've created this absolutely spectacular world that they aspire to that in most instances doesn't exist," he laments. "Then their wife, their husband, their family doesn't fit into the created mold, and they get annoyed. Expectations for perfection are way too high. Few of us are perfect. Except, of course, for Wendy."

Wendy laughs. "I hate to tell you, but he's lying," she says.

"Not that life can't be good," John continues. "My life is great. Our life is great. And it can be for everybody, but you have to be able to manage your expectations and keep them within realistic parameters. Do people live better lives? Of course, there's always somebody who has more of everything—love, money, whatever it might be. As long as you're not greedy, happiness can be found at any point in life."

These two are very satisfied with the life they've created and work they've done.

"I'm at the northern end of my career. It doesn't mean it's finished but it's getting colder," says John. He's starting to pull back on some of his professional obligations. "I'm looking forward to not going to meetings, not being on the phone, not being stressed and pulled in so many directions…," he trails off.

Looking forward to being less committed?

"Yes," he laughs. "Less committed to others and more committed to Wendy and my family." ※

Joe & Sandy Rotman | Having Fun Together

SANDY FLOUTED CONVENTION for her first date with Joe. It was October 1958. The two knew each other from growing up in the same community in Toronto. One Friday night, Joe called her up and said, "This is Joe Rotman. Would you like to go out dancing?"

"In that time," says Sandy. "You weren't supposed to go out with a guy who asked you the same day. But I just had my hair done and it was a Friday night, so I said yes."

They went out dancing. "It wasn't great," says Sandy candidly. She was tired from a week of teaching school, and Joe had brought a friend along. "They were talking philosophy to each other," says Sandy. Feeling ignored, she put her head down on the table and had a little nap.

The date got better after that. "A fellow tapped me on the shoulder and asked me to dance, which made Joe upset and he started to pay a lot of attention to me," says Sandy.

By January, they were engaged. They married in June 1959. Sandy was 21 and Joe was 23.

Joe and Sandy are devoted Canadian patriots, both sporting pins that speak to their contributions to the Great White North. On her black jacket next to a double row of brass buttons, Sandy has a flowery Order of Ontario pin, while Joe has a six-armed snowflake Order of Canada pin on his gray coat.

"It's like a knighthood," explains Sandy.

But they have room in their hearts for New York, a city they associate with their early days of marriage. They visit often, and when they do, they always stay in a suite at the Carlyle Hotel. Sitting in two armchairs, Joe looks at Sandy contentedly, a barely suppressed smile often breaking free. Behind them is a wall of windows offering a panoramic view of downtown Manhattan. A coffee table is strewn with business papers, for a trip that will mix professional meetings with a Broadway outing.

They moved to New York a few months after marrying and spent two years living on the Upper West Side, so that Joe could attend a doctorate program at Columbia Business School and Sandy could study art history. "In 1960 and 1961, we were at the center of the universe. Culture was exploding in New York," says Sandy. Joe says it was like a two-year honeymoon.

It seems in a way that the honeymoon never really ended. They both look at each other adoringly as they talk about their commitment. "I always say that people who don't get married don't want to commit, but I never thought of it as 'commitment' for myself. I just think of it as loyalty and support and we loved each other and we still do after 55 years," says Sandy, who cuts a dramatic figure with her dark glossy black hair, bronze lipstick and black leather pants.

Joe attributes their strong commitment in part to "a complementarity of their different styles." Sandy is intuitive and instinctive, while Joe is methodical with a more disciplined approach to decision-making—skills that helped him succeed in oil trading, merchant banking and investing. He was inducted into the Canadian Business Hall of Fame in 2009.

Joe says he would often seek Sandy's advice with ethical and personnel issues, because she had better judgment than him in that realm. Sandy in turn sought out Joe's advice in her philanthropy in the mental health field. His business savvy came in handy for a current project she's working on to have MBA students mentor those with mental illnesses who want to start their own businesses.

"Our different styles complement each other. She takes an idea like mental health entrepreneurs, and I can help organize it to make it happen," says Joe. "Each makes the other stronger in whatever we tackle."

Sandy's impulsive style is what led to the business school at the University of Toronto being named after Joe. "It's a very funny story," says Joe, lifting his chin toward Sandy, encouraging her to tell the tale.

Sandy explains that the University of Toronto had put Joe in charge of fundraising for the management school. Most of the people he approached, though, declined, because the business school was small at the time and not yet well-established. Sandy and Joe were at a wedding sitting at a table with the president of the university and they were talking about the difficulty raising funds. The president, Robert Prichard, asked Sandy to dance. While swirling on the dance floor, she suggested that the business school be named after Joe and that he would give the funds the school needed. When they returned to the table, Sandy kissed Joe on the cheek saying, "Congratulations."

"And then Joe said I wasn't allowed to dance with Rob Prichard ever again," says Sandy.

"We've just had a lot of fun," says Joe of their life together. "It's more that we enjoy doing things together than it is a commitment. Like when we travel, we don't travel with other couples. It's not that we don't like other people. But we are content just by ourselves."

They relate a story about one of their first trips as a couple—their real honeymoon, a six-week trip to Japan in 1959. Joe wanted to go because he was fascinated by Zen philosophy. One of his professors coordinated meetings with Zen teachers so that he could visit Zen gardens throughout the country.

"It was a different country then," says Sandy. There weren't many tourists, so young people were eager to interact with them to learn English. Sandy starts laughing. "Don't tell her the story," says Joe, who also starts laughing.

Sandy disobeys him, saying, "He's looking at stones. We've been married three weeks and he's looking at stones and looking at stones and looking at stones in these Zen gardens."

During one garden visit, two Japanese boys walked up to Sandy, who was standing alone. "May we have permission to have intercourse with you?" they asked.

"I look at Joe looking at the raked stones, and looked back at them, and said, 'Maybe,'" says Sandy. Of course, they were asking if they could have permission to speak English with her.

Joe and Sandy's styles may be different and complementary, but their senses of humor are very similar. And they share a hearty laugh together at that decades-old memory. ※

Rick & Connie Buckley | A Winning Combination

RICK AND CONNIE HAVE A CLASSIC AMERICAN HOME in Greenwich, Connecticut. Festive Christmas wreaths on gray stone pillars flank their driveway on a chilly December morning as Rick arrives in an enormous SUV. Two black standard poodles rush to greet him as he walks in the door.

In their living room is an art deco ten-cent slot machine, showing two red cherries and a yellow lemon. Its brand is Buckley—an important name to these two. "We had to have it," said Connie. Rick spotted it in an antique store in Fresno, California, while visiting one of the 20 Buckley Radio stations operated by his company.

Rick took over the family business—started in 1956—when his father died in 1972. He moved back to New York from California to assume the role of company president—and that's when he met Connie, who was working as a sales assistant at the company headquarters in Manhattan. "We, as the young kids say, got together at the Christmas holiday party," says Connie.

Some caution against workplace romances, but it worked for these two. They married less than two years later in June 1974. Connie was 25 and Rick was 36.

Thirty-eight years later, both are still at Buckley Radio, as is their only child, Jennifer. For these two, commitment, home, and work are intertwined. "Whether it's a commitment to your wife and your family, or to your business, you follow through as best you can," says Rick stoically.

Connie, wearing a black vest over a sheer flowery white blouse, adds in her high, feminine voice that it's not just a matter of blind commitment. It's important to find the right person to whom to commit. Both Rick and Connie had been married before—short marriages that they rushed into at young ages.

"In today's world, who gets married at 21?" asks Connie, reflecting on her first marriage. "You hardly know how to put one foot in front of the other."

With maturity comes an appreciation of who makes a compatible partner. "We've obviously changed as we've grown older," says Connie, but their core values have remained consistent. "We have great friends, a wonderful life, fun times—and it's all part of staying together and who we are and who we've become."

"You also learn from other people's mistakes," adds Rick. "You watch others and learn what to avoid."

For one, Rick and Connie have learned to be flexible. Connie is Greek Orthodox—she's gone to church all of her life—while Rick "doesn't really have religion on his radar screen," says Connie. Rick's approach is to enjoy life fully in the moment. "We're here a short stay," he says. This is not a point of tension for them, though. They accept and respect one other's philosophies.

Their daughter's marriage ceremony—or rather two ceremonies—reflects this easy compromise. A photo album from Jennifer's 2009 wedding to a Navy doctor sits on their living room table, next to a retrospective on Monet and Robert Kagan's Of Paradise and Power. The album has photos from both her first small ceremony for family only in the Greek Orthodox church, and from her second larger ceremony on the beach in the Hamptons.

Rick is the sailor in the family (Connie prefers tennis), but she's the one to use a sailing metaphor to describe how they react to what life throws at them. "There's this expression," she says, "You can't change the wind, but you can adjust the sails."

There have been times when the waves were rough. "We are blessed to have one child," says Rick. "We would have liked to have more but it didn't work out." He does not say this with regret. It's simply matter of fact with these two.

There are many photos of their daughter about the house. In a good number of them, she is playing hockey; she was on Boston College's team during her undergraduate years. They had hoped to also have a son. But the family adjusted to their circumstances. "Our daughter played sports for Rick," says Connie, smiling.

Rick and Connie project resilience, as if they could handle anything that comes along. "Some days are better than others. You can't just walk away after a few bad days, or even a bad year," says Connie. "Your commitment is to the family—not just to what makes you happy on a given day."

As with the Buckley slot machine, one never knows what combination one will get when pulling life's lever, but it seems like Connie and Rick hit the jackpot with one another. ※

Sadly, Rick Buckley passed away in August 2011 at the age of 74, before this book was published. We will remember him fondly.

Lear & Raquel Levin | Opposites Attract

LEAR AND RAQUEL COMPLEMENT and compliment one another. Lear is the impulsive, artistic partner. "He's the talent," says Raquel. And Raquel is the industrious, organized one. "She's a natural leader," says Lear. "And often a painfully accurate critic."

They have been partners for over four decades, both domestically and professionally. They met in 1965 at an advertising agency in Manhattan. Their first date was on Memorial Day, and by September, they were married. Lear was 24, and Raquel 21. It was impetuous, but the union has stood the test of time.

"I think you have a real good sense that you're compatible with someone right away," says Lear, a lanky man with a white beard, wearing a purple sweater. "We knew that early on and we just couldn't stay away from each other."

There was also a practical concern, says Raquel, wearing black and gray, her sparkling blue eyes smiling. Her roommate was moving out. She and Lear were together all the time, so it seemed silly not to live together. "But it was not socially acceptable at the time to do that," says Raquel.

Nowadays, it's more common for couples to live together without marrying. Lear questions that. "When it is a good fit, why prolong it?" he asks. "Tie it up. The thought of losing Raquel, I can't even contemplate that. It's too important to lose. You can't let it slip through your fingers."

They were devoted to each other early on. Perhaps that's why Raquel was open to Lear quitting his job soon after they married and spending several months searching for his dream position—Lear wanted to be a director. He got an offer in December and spent four years ascending in the field. Then in 1969, he and Raquel started their own film company, Lear Levin Productions.

Lear is named for the tragic Shakespearian king. "All my life, until I got into the film

business, I hated my name. People made fun of it," says Lear. "Then I realized that people remembered it, so it became an asset instead of something that weighed me down."

Raquel ran the business side and Lear the creative side. The mainstay of the business was national television commercials—for airlines such as United and TWA, beer companies, and car companies such as GM and Chrysler. Those commercials had Lear flying upside down in a jet plane over the Mojave Desert at 1,500 miles per hour with Chuck Yeager, almost being stampeded by a bull at a rodeo, and bailing out of a plane at 20,000 feet with the Army Rangers for a "Be All You Can Be" commercial. Lear's favorite projects, though, were documentaries, such as a feature-length film for Disney about the Ringling Brothers Circus and his work on a piece about war-torn Bangladesh, where he spent several months in 1971.

"Too long," says Raquel. She told him it was taking too long to complete.

"Even when I felt I might be making a mistake, I never felt like I couldn't do it," says Lear. "But she was right. I took too long. I tried to make it perfect and by the time it was done, the war and revolution were ancient history." He wound up donating the film to two young filmmakers who later used it in a celebrated retrospective documentary, "Song of Freedom," released in Bangladesh in 1996.

There is no bitterness over this. In Raquel and Lear's relationship, there is forgiveness and room to make mistakes. "We're very different people, extremely different people, and that's part of the attraction," says Raquel. "We always supported one another's separate work and interests."

When Raquel went off to lead consciousness-raising meetings with fellow feminists in the late 1960s, Lear was a little mystified about what went on but fully supportive. "I respected that she needed her own forum," says Lear. "In a strong relationship, it's important to not compromise your own personality too much beyond what feels healthy and to recognize that you have to allow the same thing in the other person," adds Raquel.

In preparation to talk about commitment, Raquel made notes for herself. "I found this one quote that's so precious. It's from Winnie the Pooh," she enthuses. Though they say that Raquel is the analytical one and Lear the emotional one, Raquel tears up as she reads a passage from the children's book about Piglet sidling up to Pooh to take his paw. When Pooh asks what he wants, Piglet replies, "I just wanted to be sure of you." Raquel's voice cracks and Lear rubs her back, also tearing up.

Part of commitment for them is this support—being there for each other no matter what.

"There are all different forms of commitment—to a job, to a philosophy. But with a relationship, there is a resolve to honor a third entity without mitigating the importance of the I and the you," intellectualizes Raquel. "There's this other entity that needs to be paid attention to and nurtured."

Commitment is this living and breathing entity whose presence is appreciated . . . but not analyzed at length. "If people really have to discuss it, there's something wrong with it to start with. It should be understood and explicit," adds Raquel. "With the right person, it just comes naturally."

They list the important elements of their relationship—compromise, negotiation, trust, integrity, passion, compassion, intimacy, and love for their two children. Their commitment is the foundation on which all of those elements rest.

Lear thinks his first words of commitment epitomize its meaning. "It's reflected in the marriage vows to honor and obey," says Lear. "It's a solemn pledge and in our case, it's grown stronger with time."

He gives an example. On the previous New Year's Eve, Raquel asked him to start doing some cooking. He honored the request. "I started cooking for the first time in 34 years," says Lear.

Lear has the time now. He retired from film-making a few years back, and has—partly at Raquel's urging—taken up fine-art photography. She remains his best critic, looking at a photo and identifying what's missing. "I fight criticism, but never from Raquel," says Lear. "She brings out my best side. She makes me better."

And that's of course what everyone hopes to find in a partner. ❋

Stephen & Mina Weiner | Charting a Path Together

TALKING ABOUT THEIR RELATIONSHIP in their Manhattan condo near Lincoln Center, Stephen and Mina sit on opposite ends of the couch. It's almost as if their strong personalities need extra room to be comfortable. Stephen, jocular and vivacious, says that this is an important component of their 52-year marriage.

"We give each other space," says Stephen of their allowing each other to grow over the more than five decades they've been together. They were very young when they married and have, of course, changed a lot over the years.

"You marry this person and you're either fortunate enough to grow together in parallel lines or you grow apart and diverge," says Mina. "We had a lot of luck with that."

They met in October 1957. Mina was 20 and Stephen, 23, on leave from the Army for the Jewish holidays. Stephen had recently graduated from Yale Law School and was visiting his law school roommate, Arthur Liman, in Lawrence, Long Island. Liman's mother wanted to play bridge, but they needed a fourth player. "Call that Rieur girl," she suggested.

Mina was invited over to partner with Liman's mother. "They beat us badly," says Stephen. "So I had to see her again. I couldn't let her get away with that."

During the first few months that they dated, Mina's parents were traveling in Europe to celebrate their retirement. By the time they returned, Mina and Stephen were on the path to engagement. Mina invited Stephen over for dinner to meet her parents a day after they flew back from Rome. "He was rather shy in those days," says Mina, explaining that Stephen answered every parental question with a short, direct answer, not elaborating much. "I was nervous," Stephen protests.

After Mina dropped Stephen off at the train station, she rushed home to ask her parents what they thought. "What's your hurry?" her father asked. But Mina knew what she wanted. They were engaged by March, and married in September 1958, less than a year after they met.

Stephen, a now-retired partner at Manhattan white-shoe firm Pillsbury, was a fierce litigator, but he doesn't feel the need to win every argument at home.

"When we think about our commitment, first, we both have the philosophy that we found the right person. Second, we both have the capacity to shrug off the disputes," says Stephen. Their strong personalities mean that they sometimes clash. "Neither of us is a subservient person," explains Stephen.

"But we don't clash over the serious things, more like the dishes being in the sink," says Mina. "And we don't clash overnight," adds Stephen.

Mina and Stephen do not speak over one another, but rather take turns. It seems important that each has their full say. Mina, dressed all in black with a purple pastel coat, asks, "My turn now?"

Mina was recently talking with some of her female friends about the meaning of commitment. "One of them said they thought of it as 'unwavering support.' But what if you're Mrs. Madoff?" says Mina, referring to the wife of Bernie Madoff, the stockbroker convicted in 2009 of defrauding thousands of investors of billions of dollars in a massive Ponzi scheme. "I think that you have to believe in the right ethics, and if you see the other one appears to be drifting that you feel strong enough to talk about it, and what your core values are."

Stephen and Mina share a moral compass, and each is strong enough to speak up to make sure the needle is pointed to a true ethical north. When it comes to their life maps, though, they've let one another wander into uncharted territories.

"When we got married, it was the period of *McCall's* magazine," says Mina, referring to the monthly magazine founded in 1873 dedicated to a woman's work in the home. "The woman had a good wife role to play, and the man brought home the bacon. We played that game initially with our kids. I was a stay-at-home mom. But then I decided to go back to school and conceive a career."

Stephen was supportive. Mina served as president of the Port Washington Board of Education, leaving her busy litigator husband to make dinner for himself at night. "I survived," Stephen jokes.

Mina laughs, but says seriously. "This was not the generation when husbands were expected to take that role. But I never asked and he never complained."

Mina eventually went to NYU graduate school to become a museum consultant. She has organized exhibitions for the New York Historical Society, the Museum of the City of

New York, and the South Street Seaport, among others, and wrote a book on the muralist Edwin Howland Blashfield. Mina and Stephen share a love of The Eight, a group of American artists who exhibited together in New York City in 1908. They've exhibited their collection of the realist paintings at several art museums, including that at Mina's alma mater, Cornell University.

Stephen supported Mina's desires just as she did his. After Stephen had been practicing law in New York for six years, he decided he wanted to try teaching. The law school at the University of California—Berkeley offered him a teaching position. "I never imagined living outside of New York," says Mina, but that's what Stephen wanted, so they packed up their family and moved west in 1965. "It was wild times out there then," says Stephen, who was put in charge of student conduct in a time when campus activism was experiencing a euphoric rise. They moved back to New York, and Stephen to law firm work, in 1968.

He's recently returned to teaching though, and is an adjunct professor at three New York law schools. Mina continues her museum consulting, currently working with the Institute of Classical Architecture and Classical America. "Still being active in our careers is really important," says Mina. "We both have the philosophy that idleness is the enemy of longevity," adds Stephen.

They're not idle when it comes to traveling, either. They take an exotic three-week trip every year. In the past five years, the trips have been to Vietnam, Antarctica, Egypt, Israel/Jordan, and Berlin/Prague, respectively. Australia is the only continent they haven't been to. "I'm lobbying for it," says Mina. "But that 24-hour plane trip," protests Stephen.

One gets the sense this clash will end in Mina's favor. ❋

Arthur & Diane Abbey | Intertwined

ARTHUR AND DIANE'S FIRST MEETING sounds like a scene from the movie *Grease*. It was the summer of 1954. "I picked her up on the beach," says Arthur.

Back then, all of the Long Island high school kids hung out on Jones Beach with picnic lunches, each high school partitioning off a square of sand. Diane was in her senior year at Hempstead High School and Arthur was an alumnus.

"He was a college guy and had this Pontiac convertible," says Diane, still swooning a bit after over 50 years together. Arthur was a sophomore at Hofstra College. On his trips to the Hempstead High section of the beach that summer, he kept going back to Diane's blanket. "He liked my peanut butter and jelly sandwiches," she says.

In talking about their commitment to one another, Arthur tends to focus on the caretaking aspect of their relationship. "I worry about her and take care of her, and try to make her life as pleasant as possible," he says.

That has been a theme since the very beginning. After two years of dating, in January 1957, Arthur moved to Washington, D.C. to start law school. But Diane's mother was ill, and in February, she died. "It was such a sad situation that I decided to come back to New York to be with Diane," says Arthur. He was able to switch to New York Law School.

Arthur and Diane married in June 1957; she was 19 and he was 21. They committed to each other "for richer or poorer"—those early days were the poor ones.

"We got $1,000 in wedding presents and that's all the money we had," says Arthur. They decided to spoil themselves by going on a honeymoon to Europe, sailing there on the *Queen Mary* and renting a car for a seven-week road-trip around France, Italy, and Germany. "We did it all for less than $1,000," says Arthur. They hung their clothes on the backseat of their rental car to dry and never ate a meal that came to more than $5.

They moved into a small one-room apartment in the Village, with a pull-out bed and just one window in the kitchen. They marvel at how little the rent was—$74 per month.

Thanks to Arthur's successful career in trial law, they can spend more freely these days. They now live in a beautiful, sprawling Central Park–side apartment with breathtaking art and 1,500-year-old Peruvian textiles on every available wall. Arthur excitedly shows a visitor a Peruvian poncho from 500 A.D. with diagonal, intersecting colored stripes, followed by a Lee Krasner painting filled with boxes of color. Despite the years that stretch between them, they share an underlying organizational theory. "Look," he says. "They are the same. There are no new themes."

Arthur and Diane recently left a brownstone in Gramercy Park. "We decided we needed assisted living, so we moved into a building with a doorman elevator," says Arthur, who will soon be 75.

While their life has become easier financially, their love has remained steady and consistent.

"Commitment to both of us is being together, working together, having a life together," says Diane. "And it's very much together. We're not people who go out with the guys or the girls or that kind of thing. Our interests are very similar. The commitment is a devotion to one another."

Diane and Arthur like their lives intimately intertwined. After they married, Diane raised their two children, and then taught English in the Bronx for many years. She also became a trained speaker for Planned Parenthood, speaking at schools, substance abuse centers and after-school programs. Protecting women and children is as strong a calling for her as the law is for Arthur. So the two found a way to bring their professional passions together, funding a new center at Arthur's alma mater, New York Law School, called the Diane Abbey Law Center for Children and Families.

It's not surprising that Arthur preferred to have his wife as the sole namesake for the center rather than sharing the honor. "I try very hard to put Diane ahead of me," says Arthur. "Giving towards her makes me happier than getting back."

Arthur describes it in the context of golf. Diane is his favorite golfing partner, because of the satisfaction he derives from her success on the green. "I get more joy out of seeing her hit a good shot than when I hit one," says Arthur. "Commitment's about trying to make the other person feel really good about themselves."

"It's also a sense of support to one another all the time, whatever the circumstance is, whether it's playing golf, or a problem at the office," adds Diane.

Arthur and Diane are one of those couples who are happiest thinking of each other as two halves of a whole. "We're like two people who are like one, even though we have separate bodies," says Arthur.

Like two trees planted next to one another, Diane and Arthur seem to have their roots and limbs locked together. "It's a comfortable feeling," says Diane. "If I don't know what he's doing or where he is, I'm almost uncomfortable. We've been together for a very long time. We grew up together."

"It's hard to remember not being together," says Arthur. "We've been together 80 percent of our lives."

In the best relationships, the other person's needs naturally and comfortably become your own. "I know what makes her happy and I do that," says Arthur. ❋

Michael & Kim McCarty | Excitement Without Drama

WHEN KIM FIRST MET MICHAEL, she was scared of him. "He was too loud. He was from this big Irish-American family," says Kim, a painter whose delicate and attenuated water-color children decorate the walls of their simple, modern New York apartment. "I thought I wanted a serious artist type."

Luckily, their shared love of food helped her overcome her fear. They met in the fall of 1975 in Boulder, Colorado. Kim had recently moved back to the States from Switzerland to attend the University of Colorado. Michael was majoring in gastronomy there.

In a French cooking class, the final exam was the preparation of an 18-course meal. Each student could bring a friend to help prepare his or her course. Kim was one of those helpers. Michael prepared the dessert that finished the meal. "She really liked my raspberry soufflé," says Michael.

They were both going to Los Angeles for the winter holidays to visit their parents, so their first few dates were a series of dinners together at French restaurants there. "I knew it was love at first sight because she could eat everything that she ordered, without complaining or being scared by it, like trout with the tail and the head on it," says Michael.

That spring, they moved to Los Angeles to indulge fully in the worlds of art and food. "At the time, people thought Michael was nuts to be a cook. It was a very menial position then," says Kim. Photos from the period in his cookbook, *Welcome to Michael's*, show the couple in their youthful prime—Michael, dark-haired and dashing in his cook's whites, and Kim, slim and laughing. Their life in the late 70s was a bohemian one.

"It was the beginning of the formation of new American food," says Michael. He was bringing in seeds from France for heirloom tomatoes and beets to launch the farm-to-table phenomenon in California. In 1976, he started a duck farm, and in 1979, he founded his first restaurant, Michael's Santa Monica. He was 25 and Kim was 22.

"The restaurant was like our living room. The worlds of food, wine, and art all converged there: collectors, dealers, the entertainment industry," says Michael. "And everybody who worked for us lived with us," adds Kim. Their big communal home was surprisingly full of committed relationships.

"It wasn't a swinging singles thing. Ninety percent of our friends in those days were couples, whether straight or gay," says Mike. "We didn't like to hang out with people who were going out with lots of people or cheating. It's making a commitment to a lifestyle you believe in."

And it's fortifying to be in a stable relationship. "Getting what you want to get done in a day means not having so much relationship drama in your life," adds Kim.

Kim was studying at the Art Center and collected a cohort of artist friends. And Michael's restaurant attracted creative types: the band Devo, Frank Gehry, David Hopper, Bill Bryce, Peter Alexander, David Hockney, and other artists. "That was our crowd in the 80s," says Kim.

"We met all these people who loved to do what we do, which was to have great parties and to include food, wine, and art. It was always an extravaganza," says Mike. "Hollywood was exploding with the next generation."

Kim and Michael got married in 1984, and had their two children in the late 80s. They began commuting back and forth between California and New York when Michael opened a second restaurant in Manhattan in 1989. It also attracted creative types and has become especially popular among the publishing crowd. Michael has just come from breakfast, where Tina Brown, editor of *The Daily Beast*, and formerly of *Vanity Fair* and *The New Yorker*, was holding court.

Being in the restaurant business means crazy hours. Michael is there for all three meals. "Of all our restaurant friends, no one has stayed married," says Kim.

How did they make it work? "You have to have faith, and be stubborn," says Kim. "Commitment is give and take," adds Michael. "Some people are stubborn in the wrong way and can't do that, and then their commitment ends."

Kim's studio in New York is across the street from the restaurant, which is a walkable distance from their apartment. She'll often duck in at lunch for a cup of soup. In California, they're more spread out. Their house in Malibu is on a vineyard overlooking the ocean. "We get a break from both cities, and we get the buzz of both cities," says Michael of their bicoastal life.

"Commitment is about being flexible, and staying focused on what you need, but being able to roll with the punches. Say if the in-laws suddenly show up at the door," says Kim. Or if your house burns down, as Michael and Kim's did in the Malibu fires of 1993.

"It's very joyful. I love that I've been with the same woman for 35 years. What we see in our friends—men and women alike—is the pain and suffering of not finding someone you love to be with all the time," says Michael.

Being in the midst of a vibrant restaurant community means encountering many celebrities and power hitters. "Some people are hot and happening and take it so seriously," says Kim. "The next minute they're down in the dumps. Who's going to stick by them?"

Michael and Kim have stuck by each other, and they focus on the high times rather than the low ones. "We have a good time together," says Michael. "That's what's important." ※

Joan Gelman & Don Aronson | Second Act

JOAN AND DON HAVE THE CONVERSATIONAL RHYTHM of two professional comedians. After all, they've honed their act over 25 years of marriage.

It was a second marriage for both of them, Joan having divorced at a young age and Don widowed. "He had a great marriage. I did not," says Joan, who was single for many years after her divorce. When her girlfriends asked what kind of man she was looking for, she would say, "I like a guy like Don Aronson. He wears corduroy pants and has a great sense of humor," says Joan. "He was my type of guy. But he was happily married."

When he became widowed, Joan acted. "That's the one I want," she thought at the time. She looks at Don lovingly. "And I really nailed him!"

On this sunny November morning, Don is not in corduroy pants. The former accounting executive who now has his own consulting business, is wearing dark pants with a checkered shirt. Joan is wearing all black, with a cream-colored satin shirt under a sweater. She prefers standing to sitting. "I have too much energy," she says. Their sun-filled living room is like a giant curio cabinet: on one table is a coin-operated automat from the 50s offering a bologna sandwich or a piece of cherry pie for three nickels. A display case holds ashtrays and drink holders from New York's famous Stork Club, which closed down in the early 60s. High on one wall above their fireplace is an antique porcelain-faced clock from a French train station in the Franche-Comte region. "It doesn't work," says Don, helpfully.

The couple shares a love of collecting antique mechanical objects and advertising materials from the 30s, 40s, and 50s. "I love history and nostalgia," says Joan, a television producer, who co-authored a book on the topic, *How to Set Up for Mah-Jongg and Other Lost Arts*.

"You've got to have the recreation part in common," says Joan of one important element of a second marriage.

"The first time you get married, there's no history or baggage. You're open to being molded," adds Don. "For the second marriage, there's history and baggage to be reconciled." It helps then to have many similarities and likes, as Joan and Don do: traveling, politics, movies, ballet, theater, collecting, attending auctions. "And we both hate opera," says Don.

During their first marriages, Joan and Don lived in the same New Jersey suburban community and had known each other for many years. They lived in different towns but were neighbors at the hospital for the births of Don's first daughter and Joan's second son. Their rooms being next door to each other and their children being born at approximately the same time led to a little confusion. When a nurse brought a newborn baby into Joan's room, she only realized it was Don's daughter when the nurse went to cut off her wristband just before she was about to take her home.

Joan had married right after graduating from college in the late 1950s. "In those days, you got married because you were graduating from college. If you didn't, you were an old maid," she says.

The marriage lasted just two and a half years, and Joan spent the next couple of decades raising her two sons and developing her producing career at ABC, NBC, and CBS. She always liked Don and so when she realized he was single, she asked her college roommate (our *Commitment* photographer's wife) Joan Hamburg to invite Don onto her radio show to talk about Ronald Reagan's tax cuts. When Don asked how Hamburg got his name, she said it was through Joan Gelman.

Don called Joan to thank her and asked her to go to the ballet with him that Saturday. They went out again the following Saturday, moved in together six weeks later in 1985, and married six months later in January of 1986. At their wedding, Don's daughter gave a toast: "Joan tried to steal me 25 years ago and now she finally has me."

"People ask me what I liked about Joan," says Don. "I say: A brother-in-law who had parking garages and a rent-stabilized apartment."

They joke a lot, but they're very much in love. "I was insanely out of my mind over him," says Joan.

In Joan, Don found someone whose accomplishments he respected and whose company he craved. "Commitment makes you a full person. It's part of your identity," says Don.

And companionship is important—for humans and for animals. When Joan got a dog, Don insisted they get another so they could play together. "Our puppy was lonely and sleeping all day," says Don.

"So now we have two dogs that sleep all day," says Joan.

Joan and Don are at ease together—their dogs, love, and shared interests making their lives richer and fuller.

"If somebody told me I had to do something for the next 40 years, no matter how passionate I was about it, it would be daunting," says Joan. "For me, it's day by day. I don't feel locked in."

"Not that we're promiscuous," interjects Don. Joan mock scowls, laughing.

"I'm doing what I want to do and I want to be with him," says Joan. "Commitment doesn't bind you. It frees you." ※

Arnon & Eileen Lambroza
Working Together to Achieve Happiness

FOR ARNIE AND EILEEN, it really was love at first sight. Or love at first communal work-out.

The two met at a Philadelphia gym in 1987, when Eileen, then 24, was a medical student and Arnie, then 27, was a medical resident. Eileen, petite with fine, pretty features and shoulder-length brown hair, remembers being struck by her now-husband's eyes when he looked up while pulling a weight bar down toward his shoulders.

"I saw Eileen and I felt an instant attraction," says Arnie, who bears a passing resemblance to George Clooney with his salt-and-pepper hair and dark, soulful eyes. "I felt a little heart flutter. I thought, 'Wow, she's really good-looking. Why can't I meet someone like that?'"

He worked up the courage to ask her out on a date and they discovered that there was more between them than simple chemistry. "I was really excited that she was a person who was really attractive and in medicine—an unusual combination," says Arnie. "Physical attraction only gets you so far. When you start thinking about spending your life with somebody, it has to be someone you respect and feel is an equal—intellectually and in terms of goals in life. Everything seemed to fall into place that way."

The two got engaged a year later at the River Café in Brooklyn—even though Arnie almost dropped the ring in the river—and were married at the end of 1988.

Post-work on a weekday on the Upper East Side of New York, the Lambrozas are both wearing their white doctor's coats after spending the day with patients. Both have carefully written out their definitions of commitment on Post-It Notes.

Eileen's note contains two sentences in neat, bubbly writing, the final one ending with a perky exclamation point: "It's unconditional love. It's when your happiness, dreams, and life goals are forever entwined—and with the right person, it's absolutely the best!"

"Mine's a little sloppier," says Arnie. His note is in a cursive that leans harrowingly toward the right on some lines: "Commitment means devoting yourself to someone, giving them your absolute trust and love, and working together to achieve happiness."

That last clause can be taken literally. Eileen and Arnie share an office for their separate medical practices. She is a dermatologist and he is a gastroenterologist. White orchids greet visitors in the shared reception area of their Park Avenue office. In addition to the usual magazines—*InStyle*, *New York*, *Glamour*, *Vogue*, *MotorTrend*—the reception area has books on Italian frescoes and Leonardo Da Vinci, because the Lambrozas love Italian and Renaissance art. Before having their two children, they traveled around Italy, to see the Uffizi gallery in Florence, among other destinations. Arnie's office has reconstructed buildings from Florence, including the Campanile and the Duomo—built from kit models.

Though don't be fooled by their last name. Arnie is actually descended from Sephardic Jews who lived in Russia. "Though, if you go far enough back, the Italian side must be in the genetic code somewhere," says Lambroza.

Since they share an office, Eileen and Arnie get more time together than most married couples. They moved in together (professionally) in August 1997, shortly before the birth of their son. Their current office is just six blocks from their home, meaning it's easy for their teen children to pop in regularly. "Somebody told me you have to keep everything within ten blocks in New York," says Eileen.

"Some couples thrive on having a lot of separation. But we're the opposite," says Arnie. "We spend a lot of time together and like to spend a lot of time together."

"We see each other a lot, but we're still excited about it," adds Eileen. "It's really fun to see him throughout the day and to be able to say hi."

When they speak, they fall into a comfortable pitter-patter, easily picking up where the other leaves off.

"We have very similar outlooks. We're both reasonable. We don't like to stay angry at each other or others for very a long period of time," says Arnie. "We're not stubborn. We don't hold grudges. The fact that we're both like that is a nice thing about the relationship, and helps us deal with stressful times."

"We get along really well," says Eileen simply.

"Some couples work because of their differences, but we work well because we are so similar," adds Arnie. ※

Allan & Sondra Gotlieb | Lucky in Love

ON ALLAN AND SONDRA'S WEDDING DAY, they admit that they barely knew each other. They had spent only a handful of days together.

They met at a friend's house in Winnipeg in 1955 when Sondra was 17 and Allan was 27. She brought him a dish of ice cream during a game of chess. "She was very beautiful—a beautiful face, complexion, and figure," says Allan, who was leaving 10 days later, to return to a donship at Oxford.

He sent her long letters from England—"Boring letters, describing the buildings there," says Sondra—and called her a month after his return to propose. "I said yes because I didn't want to go to university and it was a great opportunity to travel. I didn't think about marriage very much. I thought I had a good travel guide," says Sondra. "It wasn't that romantic but maybe that's the way things should be."

When Allan returned to Canada that winter, they barely recognized one another. "I couldn't remember him. I had lost weight and he didn't recognize me. And we got married," says Sondra. (This later inspired Sondra to write a book, *True Confections: How My Family Arranged My Marriage*, which won the Stephen Leacock humor prize in 1979.)

"Even for that time, it was extraordinary for how fast it was and how little we knew each other," says Sondra.

It may not have been the most romantic start, but the two fell deeply in love over the years and have led a most-romantic life since as world diplomats. This December afternoon marks their fifty-fifth anniversary. They are visiting New York, with reservations for the evening at La Grenouille.

Allan in a gray suit with blue pinstripes and dark-rimmed glasses, wearing an order of Canada pin on his lapel, did prove to be an adept travel guide. "A world opened up," says Sondra. The newlyweds toured Europe while based at Oxford, and a year later, returned to Canada where Allan started working in the Diplomatic Service. His postings took them to Geneva, Ottawa, and Washington, D.C. When they lived in Ottawa, Sondra traveled across Canada, picking up regional recipes from food shops and pastry shops and writing two cookbooks.

Their favorite posting was in the United States, when Allan served as Canadian ambassador from 1981 to 1989, during the Reagan years. "The good years," says Sondra.

It was a glorious time for the couple. "It was breathlessly exciting. We met everybody in the world in D.C.," says Sondra. Their extravagant parties at the Canadian embassy were legendary.

Sondra, dressed in black with short honey-colored hair, was a more visible figure than most diplomats' wives. She authored a column for the *Washington Post* called "Wife of…"

"At all the luncheons and events we went to, wives were introduced as 'The wife of so and so,'" explains Sondra. "Women were appendages in that kind of political environment," says Allan. "The only time wives were important in Washington was when their husbands betrayed them."

Both wrote books about those years in D.C.: Allan's was titled *Washington Diaries* detailing his meetings with the luminaries of the day and Sondra's was *Washington Rollercoaster.* Now based back in Toronto, Sondra writes a column for the *National Post,* and Allan is an advisor to a leading law firm.

One of their children calls Allan on his cell phone to wish his parents a happy 55th anniversary. How did they know this would all turn out so well in those early days when they barely knew each other?

"The glue formed after the marriage," says Allan. "Though we were both committed to making it work. Our cultural milieu was that marriage was an enduring commitment."

Allan says he was in love with Sondra from the very beginning, though he recognized that she was young and thus still relatively unformed in many ways. "I thought she was very intelligent and perceptive, and that she would continue to develop into an interesting and exciting person," he says.

"I wasn't madly in love when we got married," admits Sondra. "I looked up to my husband and he liked it. Fortunately, our personalities clicked. The love grew."

"Maybe we were just lucky," says Allan.

Allan and Sondra prove that being lucky and being committed to commitment are an excellent combination for a long, lasting, and loving marriage. ❋

Abigail Pogrebin & David Shapiro | Taken for Granted

ABBY AND DAVE MET ON A BLIND DATE. "It was surprising," says Abby. "Because I'm a cynical New Yorker who believes blind dates don't work out."

An office-mate of Dave's had set them up. They met at a restaurant on the Upper West Side. "It was effortless from the first moment I sat down," says Abby.

She was working as a producer for Ed Bradley at *60 Minutes*, while Dave was in finance, having moved to New York four years earlier, after business school at the University of Chicago to work in private equity.

"When you go on blind dates, you kind of know in the first minute or two whether it's going to work out," says Dave. They clicked immediately. "We knew something bigger than just a decent date had happened."

"I remember that his questions were interesting," says Abby. Since she comes from a family of journalists, that's an especially important trait. Her mother, Letty Cottin Pogrebin, co-founded *Ms.* magazine. Her twin sister is a culture reporter for the *New York Times*. Abby is a magazine writer and has authored two books: *Stars of David: Prominent Jews Talk About Being Jewish* and *One and the Same: My Life as an Identical Twin and What I've Learned About Everyone's Struggle to Be Singular*.

That initial blind date was in February 1993. They moved in together in May, got engaged in October, and married in December. "And there was no shotgun involved," says Dave.

They say it moved quickly because of their ages; Dave was 31 and Abby, 28. "At that age, you know when it feels right," says Dave, now a managing partner at the private equity firm he co-founded, KPS Capital Partners.

Abby liked that Dave wasn't a New Yorker. "He's the most genuine person I've ever known," she says. "There is no artifice, even when you might want some."

Dave may have the sincerity of a Midwestern upbringing, but his life with Abby now is very New York. Up until just recently, they lived on the Upper West Side with their two children in the historic Ansonia, a beautiful old building that began its life as a luxury hotel—its condos have been the cinematic home for fictional Manhattanites such as Jennifer Jason Leigh and Bridget Fonda's roommates in *Single White Female* and Halle Berry's news reporter in *Perfect Stranger*.

Both lanky and fit, Abby and Dave pair well together. Sitting on their couch, a crisp November air filling the room thanks to propped windows, Abby leans forward as she talks in a raspy voice, while Dave leans back and tends to let his wife lead the conversation.

Abby says that her relationships before meeting Dave were volatile, full of conflict and overdramatic break-ups. She thought that's what she needed to keep a relationship from being boring. But in Dave, she found someone whose opinions are always surprising, but with whom she doesn't clash. They say that in their almost 18 years of marriage they've never had a serious, screaming fight.

"I don't need Dave to be a circus," says Abby. "He constantly interests and challenges me, but I don't need him to be a color light show every day. I just needed a person to keep me clear on what matters. He steadies me in a way that I now see I needed."

"We complement each other," says Dave. "Abby is play-by-play and I'm color commentary."

They may be different in their conversational styles, but when it comes to key decisions, they are like-minded, especially when it comes to their children, Benjamin, 14, and Molly, 12.

"We were both hit by parenthood the same way. We were deeply in love with each other, and it was tenfold for our children," says Abby. "That's not always simple. When a parent is smitten with a child, sometimes a spouse will say, 'What about me?' We both had the same reaction of falling in love with our kids and wanting them to be primary. It's not at the exclusion of our relationship, but they take precedence. And we share in the delight of that."

Both were able to look to their parents for examples of a strong and healthy commitment. (Abby's parents were profiled in the first book in this series—*Couples: A Celebration of Commitment*.) Like Abby and Dave, their parents in both cases met and married within a year. Those two decades-long marriages are "rock solid." "Coming from that strong base clearly informed our choice of each other," says Abby.

"To me, commitment is an unquestioning, a lack of conditionality," says Dave. "When you first commit to each other, you know that your partner will evolve and change, but you're committing to changing together and respecting those changes."

In addition to the potential for change, there's an acceptance of one another's flaws, says Abby. "It would be fair for Dave to point out my neurotic tendencies—and to make more of them," says Abby. But she says that would likely make them worse. Dave not pointing them out, minimizes them. "My own flaws and insecurities would be reified if Dave made more of them. But they don't matter to him. He appreciates them as quirks. I think commitment in a way is making each other feel like we are our best selves. There's no false building up, but there's just this tremendous base of unquestioned belief in each other."

"You don't take for granted the love and support, but you do in a way," Dave says. "You know it will be there and it makes you stronger. It makes me feel better and allows me to go out and live my life outside my family the way I do. I can move confidently through my day knowing that I have that sure base at home."

Abby and Dave are somewhat perplexed by people that describe marriage as work. "There are plenty of things in life we have to work at," says Dave. "Hopefully, the most important relationship in your life is one that doesn't require that kind of work. By its nature, by the fact of it, hopefully it takes care of itself." ❊

Marty & Linda Greenhouse
Love Dies When Lovers Want It To

LINDA AND MARTY SEEM TO BE CONNECTED by an invisible tether. When in the same room, they don't tend to drift more than a few feet away from one another, and it's obvious that they delight in the pull of that indiscernible cord.

"We were just listening to our answering machine, and every message starts, 'Hi Linda and Marty,'" says Marty. "Although you have your own beliefs, dreams and aspirations, you start looking at the two of you as one unit. You think of yourself as 'us.'"

Life becomes defined by "how things affect the two of you and not just yourself," adds Linda. The two are sitting together in the living room of their Upper East Side home, surrounded by Asian art, including a large painting with red lettering done by the Emperor's calligrapher and a sizeable collection of small Tang Dynasty figurines. (They haven't yet visited Asia, but they appreciate the aesthetic.)

They met in 1970 as undergraduates at Pennsylvania State University when their respective roommates started dating. "They split, and we stuck," says Marty. They married in 1973 when both were 22. Linda stayed home to raise their daughter and son, while Marty built a career in advertising.

They talk about their commitment as a multiplier of the beautiful moments in life and a dispeller of the difficult ones. "Commitment is being there to share everything. You have to be a good sharer," says Marty. "And you grow accustomed to that sharing so that when you experience something without the other person, the joy is not as joyous, and the pain is more painful."

"It's comforting to know that if you're going through something difficult, you can collapse into the arms of the other person," says Linda. "And at the same time, you want to be there and be strong when your partner is going through something difficult."

Looking back on their life, the difficult times don't leap out, though. There were

tough times, they say, but only in a financial sense, when their two children were young and Marty first started his advertising company. Linda would make huge lasagna meals to last the family a week. "Those times didn't bring out bitterness or arguments," says Linda. "It wasn't a problem in the marriage. We were in it together."

Marty built a large, successful advertising agency, which he sold to the Interpublic Group of Companies 12 years ago. He recently started a new one, Bg Two. "I'm a worker bee," he says of his decision not to retire. After their children left home—their daughter and son are in their 30s now—Linda got a master's degree in art education. She's now head of the art department at a day school in Westchester County.

These two are hyper aware of one another. They can tell if something is bothering the other with a simple look. And they will immediately discuss it. "We don't feel happy if the other person isn't happy," says Linda. They do not like tension in their home—which is part of the reason they are drawn to the simple, clean lines of Chinese calligraphy and peaceful landscape scenes for the artwork they own.

When talking about how "commitment" is perceived today by younger generations, they see upsides and downsides.

"Before, in our parents' time, people stayed together for lots of different reasons—kids, money, family pressure, societal expectations. I think today people stay together because they *want* to stay together," says Marty.

That ease with which people can enter into and slip out of commitments now, though—thanks to societal acceptance of living together unmarried and of divorce—means that some people enter into relationships too easily and recklessly, knowing there is an out.

"When we were growing up, marriage was what you did if you wanted to stay with someone. Otherwise, society frowned on you," says Linda. "And when I was a kid, if someone's parents got divorced, that was seen as disgraceful. And they became outsiders, especially the woman. But now divorce is so much more prevalent, and people consider that option from when they first form the relationship. They don't necessarily feel like they're going into it forever."

That leaves the door open for a constant questioning of the relationship, rather than a resolve to make commitment work.

"Let's face it. Today, a lot of people go into marriages with pre-nups, and that presupposes that there's a possibility they might get divorced," adds Marty. "We never thought in a million years when we got married that divorce was an option."

When Linda thinks about commitment, she thinks back to a song that Marty composed for her on her 40th birthday, titled, "What Happens To Love." Linda quotes a meaningful line from the song: "Love dies when lovers want it to."

"That's a very true thought," she says. "As long as you both really want the relationship and are willing to fight for it, it will survive."

But one gets the sense that these two don't have to fight for it. More than survive, their love thrives from their commitment being woven through with the strong threads of mutual admiration and adoration. Marty says that they still feel young together, their love fresh, quoting another line from the song: "When I see lovers, know what I see? I still see you and I still see me." ❋

Bert & Gloria Abrams | A Classical Story

BERT AND GLORIA HAVE FRÉDÉRIC CHOPIN TO THANK for their 52-year marriage. The two met on a blind date in November 1956, set up by one of Gloria's sorority sisters. Gloria was in her final year of college and Bert in his final year of law school.

"When I took her home that night, I didn't think I was going to call her again," said Bert, who explains that in those days it was common to go on lots of first dates but not often on second ones. "I was driving my father's car, and the radio was tuned to WQXR, a classical music station. I thought I knew classical music quite well, but as I was dropping her off, a piece of music came on that I didn't recognize."

Gloria knew it to be a Chopin piece, and that was a sign for Bert that she might be special. So he asked her out again the next week to accompany him to a law school dinner dance.

"I later learned that she happened to play that piece on the piano growing up. But I was impressed with her knowledge," says Bert, a senior adviser at a private equity firm. He doesn't smile easily, but his face fills with joy at that memory.

"It was fate that the radio station played that," adds Gloria, sitting beside Bert on the couch in their salmon-walled living room on the Upper East Side. Opera music drifts in from their bedroom down the hall, where the radio is again tuned to WQXR. "That's from *South Pacific*," says Gloria, still quick on the music trivia draw. "And I didn't play that one growing up!"

After law school, Bert joined the Army reserves and was stationed in Fort Dix in New Jersey. Gloria visited him there every weekend that he was unable to go to New York. "The devotion was building," she says.

"We never talked a lot about getting married," says Bert. "We just did. We were together for a certain number of years and it became inevitable."

They got married in February 1959. Though Bert's phrasing is not romanticized, the tenderness he feels toward his wife is evident in their interaction and his gaze toward her. For him, commitment is conveyed in action, not in words.

"We never over the years talked a lot about commitment," says Bert. "We raised two children, experienced the vicissitudes of life, and just lived life together without talking about it a lot. We have friends who have a lot of conversations about their commitment, but we never did that. We just did commitment. Commitment becomes a natural, unspoken fact, enhanced by shared experiences over the years."

Gloria describes Bert as her best friend. She says that they actually did have many, many conversations, just not about the ins and outs about the nature of their commitment, per se. "Part of our strength is that we both felt we could talk to each other when something bothered us, rather than letting it bottle up," says Gloria. "We always explore things that trouble us about our relationship or things that we are happy about. It's funny that people don't tend to talk about the things that make them happy. People are more likely to talk about what disturbs them, but people should really talk about both."

Bert and Gloria express some surprise that other couples feel the need to talk about each other with outsiders. They never desired that, due to the open channel of communication between them. "I never felt like I needed to talk about Bert with others. I would just talk to him," says Gloria.

For these two, commitment is about "being there for each other in good and bad times," says Gloria. "In 52 years together, you learn to be part of each other's lives. It is not totally smooth. You have your bumps, but you learn from them."

Gloria focused on raising their two children. When their kids grew older, she and Bert talked about the fact that she wanted to do something outside of the home. She found a volunteering opportunity at the Metropolitan Museum, and started working there in 1972. "It really enhanced her life," says Bert. She decided to go to graduate school to get her master's. "We and the kids went through her master's together," says Bert, who says the children pitched in and made dinners.

"It strengthened our relationship," says Bert. "Because she had an independent activity to match my own."

It made them equals, their love and commitment commingled with mutual respect.

They can't now remember the name of the Chopin piece that set them on their happy lifelong course together. Bert shakes his head, still in disbelief that chance and Chopin made him ask Gloria out on the second date that eventually led to marriage, children, grandchildren, and a loving partnership.

"Of those little incidents, lives are made," says Bert. "What would have happened if I'd been listening to WNYC instead WQXR?" ※

Peri Wolfman & Charlie Gold | Paired Well Together

THE TALE OF CHARLIE AND PERI'S MEETING and their eventual courtship years later would provide a pleasant plot device for a feel-good family movie. They first met in 1966 at a dinner party celebrating Charlie's mother getting engaged to the father of Peri's then-husband.

Peri and her then-husband had a one-year-old, and Charlie was just on the brink of getting married. They became part of one big extended family, seeing each other at holiday gatherings and big events.

"We were family for a very long time. We celebrated Thanksgiving, Christmases and children's birthdays together," says Peri, who has curly black hair with a striking gray streak in the bangs. "We had always liked each other a lot and were very good friends."

Peri was based in California, while Charlie was in New York. Their marriages both led to the birth of two sons, but also to divorce. Divorces can lead to fractures in a big family, if sides are chosen and family members alienated, but that iciness had not established itself in this case. When Peri was on a business trip to New York, she was comfortable with reaching out to Charlie when she needed a favor. She had to have some film developed, and knew that Charlie, a renowned food photographer, was the man who could help her do it. He went to great lengths to help her, and she took him to lunch to thank him.

"And that was it. We were just absolutely crazy about each other and fell in love," says Peri. The wheels began turning quickly on their romance. Peri and her two sons, aged 14 and 12, moved from California into Charlie's house in Manhattan in 1980. Charlie's sons, then 10 and 9, lived with their mother and visited on weekends. Though they moved in together, they didn't get married. That would come later. Many years later.

Their four sons were already friends—"They already knew each other. They were cousins," says Peri—but the first year was filled with fighting as they figured out the new

hierarchy. Once that was established, they got into lots of mischief: paper airplanes that the boys would set on fire and throw down from the terrace of their Gramercy Park apartment; frozen bottles of vodka in the freezer because too much of the vodka had been replaced with water; and a washer and dryer that kept breaking, because the boys wanted to see what the spin cycle was like with one of them inside.

"We went through raising our boys together," says Peri.

These days, Charlie and Peri, both 71, live in a high-ceilinged, light-filled apartment in SoHo. It used to be Charlie's studio, but they transformed it into a living space when he gave up working as the industry changed from analog to digital photography. Charlie wears round glasses, and laughs and smiles easily remembering their sons' hijinks. Peri's gray-green eyes twinkle, though she seems more scandalized than amused remembering the boys' tricks.

This is part of how the couple functions. "We have a lot of tumult in our life, which we like—children, grandchildren, dogs, dinner parties," says Peri. The sense of taking care of all these things together is part of their commitment. "The commitment is to the relationship, the family and the lifestyle. It's not just to each other but to your life together."

She quotes from an article she read recently about why people always need to have dogs about. "'In order to stay young, you must always have something annoying at your feet.' That's why we keep getting dogs," she says. "That sense of responsibility and commitment keeps us going. We have differences, but the bottom line is that we really care about these creatures—the dogs and the children and the grandchildren."

Besides creature comforts (and discomforts), Peri and Charlie's commitment is rooted in the things they've created together. They love cooking and spending time in the kitchen. In 1981, Peri opened a home furnishing store, Wolfman-Gold Good Company.

"That's what my store looked like," she says, gesturing at their open kitchen with white walls and white dishes stacked on open white shelves rather than in cabinets. "A clean white space," adds Charlie. "There was nothing like it at the time."

The two started collaborating on books. The first was *The Perfect Setting*. "It was perfect. I ran a table-top store and Charlie was a table-top photographer," says Peri, who's now working on a dinner collection for Restoration Hardware.

They lived, loved, and worked together for 16 years before getting married. In 1996, they threw a surprise wedding at their second home in the Hamptons. They invited the whole family to join them for Labor Day weekend. "No one asked me why I was baking a cake with white icing in my bathing suit," says Peri.

Why did they wait so long? "We had a wonderful relationship. We weren't going to have children. We shared everything," Charlie says. It wasn't until they started thinking about caring for each other as they aged that they started worrying about legally being empowered to do that.

"It was kind of cool not to be married. We were like married people. We did everything together. We owned everything together," says Peri, who admits marriage wasn't a priority for them when they met as they were both coming out of divorces. "We had our weddings. What's the difference if you live together or you're married unless you're young and forming a family?"

"When you're living together and you're not married, you may be nicer to each other. You realize the other could more easily leave," says Charlie. "I think back on our relationship and there we were living together, sharing everything with no legal paperwork, just love. That to me is commitment. We were committed to do for each other. If she fell down, I would help her up, and vice versa. Surgeries, all those things you go through, we are there for each other with love and affection."

"In this day and age, you can walk away from anything," adds Peri. "Commitment means that when someone has a problem or is going through something difficult, you stay with them and help them work through it."

She then refers to Charlie's professional identity crisis, as he retires from photography. "It's harder for men than women to give up a career of 45 years," she says. "Women can slide from one career to another and reinvent themselves, but men don't have that mentality. When they give up what they've done their whole lives, it's a challenge."

A challenge they're committed to overcoming. Life may get turbulent at times, but these two are there to steady each other no matter how hard the wind blows. ❊

Norbert & Judy Weisberg | Loyalty, Respect, and an Agreement to Disagree

NORBERT AND JUDY WERE FIXED UP BY FRIENDS TWICE, though neither understood why the first time.

That first disastrous meeting was in 1983, at a dinner party arranged by Norbert's cousin. Norbert had been told that Judy was a redhead so he immediately spotted her when he walked in; she was chatting with Leonard Weinglass, the lawyer known for representing the Chicago Seven in the 1960s.

"I walked over to the couch and introduced myself, and she blew me off, perfunctorily," says Norbert. He was insulted and signaled to his cousin that she should introduce him to someone else. During the dinner, Norbert's cousin, her fiancé, and Judy, who were all psychoanalysts, spent the whole night talking about the field. Norbert tried again to engage Judy, jokingly saying, "I can't believe you all talk shop all day long." She ignored that. "So I left the party and intended never to see her again," says Norbert.

Six months later, another matchmaking friend of his said she'd met a woman who was "very suitable" for him. The friend spent five minutes lauding the mystery match before Norbert asked what her name was. It was Judy again. "I said, 'Under no circumstances will I meet with her.' My friend insisted, and out of pure beneficence I decided to do that."

That date went far better. "Judy is a pretty perfunctory person—she makes decisions quickly," says Norbert. "I guess the second time she heard more out of my mouth than hello and decided it was worth listening to."

They married two years later, in 1985. It was a second marriage for both of them, and each had grown children from their first marriages.

Sitting at the dining room table in their high-ceilinged West Village home, Norbert, a chairman of two corporate boards, is sporting a blue-checkered button-up shirt. He is a large presence, easily surpassing six feet tall, with gray hair and kind blue eyes. Judy, who now works as a psychologist, is physically his opposite. She is petite, wearing a black and brown wavy-patterned shirt. She has unruly short brown hair and dark eyes, which are conveying a bit of exasperation at the moment.

Usually, it seems that it is men who are not keen to talk about commitment, but in this interview, it is Judy who is initially reluctant to open up. She describes the meaning of commitment as "loyalty, support and respect," and stops there.

Norbert elaborates: "It's a feeling of incontrovertible reliability. It's being able to talk to Judy about things that I would not necessarily be able to easily talk to other people about."

He says Judy is one of the few people who is able to draw him out. "When there are problems, she is good at talking about how those problems make her feel and why," he says. "That lubricates my ability to respond and to talk about the subject."

That is when Judy warms to the topic. She explains that commitment in a second marriage differs, in that it requires a heightened respect for genuine differences of opinion. Meeting at an older age means that there's less of the merging of the selves, since those selves are so indelibly formed. "We have a lot of divergent interests," says Norbert.

They were both quite accustomed to their independence. After all, Judy was single for 15 years and Norbert was single for 10 years before they married.

"It's not just respecting each other's differences and interests," adds Judy. "There are issues where we feel very differently about things. We respect that."

Judy mentions the settlements in the West Bank as an example of one of these issues. "I'm against and he's for," says Judy.

"That's oversimplifying it," interjects Norbert. "I'm not 'for' settlements, but I'm for understanding the Israeli position on settlements."

The fact that they don't have to agree on everything is an important point, says Judy. "You have to identify where you are not going to be able to persuade the other and not waste time on it," she says. This does not just apply to political disagreements. "We each have two children, and between us, eight grandchildren," she says. "We can have very strong differences on what's healthy and not healthy for their development, and we just make an agreement not to argue about it."

While they may have healthy disagreements, love and comfort underlies it all. "We come home to one another both seeking succor," says Norbert. "We may disagree sometimes, but we're frequently bothered by the same things and respect the same things. That's part of what drew us to one another, and it perpetuates the commitment."

They were also drawn to each other out of admiration. Judy notes that her husband is the chairman of two companies because they needed a leader. "They needed someone smart, and Norby is very smart," she says.

Norbert takes equal pride in his wife. "I have a lot of respect for Judy. I get a lot of pleasure seeing her out there among other people, and comparing her with other people, and she always comes out favorably in those comparisons," he says.

They depend on each other, and increasingly appreciate the unfailing support of the other as they age. "I know she is there for me," says Norbert. "I know that if I get into trouble—no matter how flighty or serious the trouble is—she is there with advice. She really cares about my well-being. There aren't that many people who care with that intensity—including children. And there never will be. It's naïve to expect children—with their own lives, children, husbands, and wives—will ever be able to afford the affection that you sometimes need. But Judy is there all the time."

That's intimacy for them, says Judy—this deep well of caring.

To her earlier catalogue of the components of commitment, Judy now adds trust: "Trust that you can count on being understood, and trusting that the other will give an honest point of view, without withdrawing affection."

Commitment is that: the trust that your partner will reliably be there for you, with love, honesty, respect, support, and the occasional disagreement. ❊

Michael Tucker & Jill Eikenberry
Complete Transparency

MICHAEL TUCKER AND JILL EIKENBERRY famously played the part of married attorneys for eight years on the television show *L.A. Law.* Their off-screen marriage spans a much longer period, and started years before they got the gig as one of the most memorable couples in legal drama.

If you ask them how they met, you'll likely get an incredibly candid response. "We met and had an affair," says Michael. "I was married."

"I was engaged," adds Jill.

Honesty, even when brutal, is the bedrock of the two actors' four-decade-long marriage. Communication is an essential skill for their craft, so it may not be surprising that they are able to articulate difficult truths. But they've also gone to great lengths—including attending tantric classes and studying with a guru—in order to ensure that every line of communication is open between them.

They met in 1970, both working as stage actors at the Arena Stage in Washington, D.C. Jill, then 25, was fresh out of Yale Drama School, while Michael, then 27, had four years of regional theater experience, as well as a wife and a one-year-old daughter.

"It wasn't a good idea to feel the feelings we were feeling, but it was fairly undeniable," says Jill, a striking blonde with delicate features who looks down on her shorter husband even while wearing simple black athletic sneakers. Michael has close-cut white gray hair, wire-framed glasses, and a smile that's not easily repressed for long.

"I think it was a dalliance to Mike," continues Jill. "But I knew from the beginning that it was bigger than my ability to control the situation."

When the show season was over, they had to either end the affair or escalate it.

"I moved in with Jill, and left my wife and year-old daughter," says Michael. "A couple of weeks later, my then-wife came to us and offered my daughter Alison to us. She said,

'You're happy, I'm not.' I thought that was a brave thing to do."

"I looked at Jill," continues Michael, "who was young and maybe not thinking that was the path for her life, and she said okay."

"That was a moment of commitment right there," says Jill.

These were not easy decisions to make, and they were not made lightly, but it was clear to them that they had to be together.

"That clarity created a glue for us throughout all these years," says Jill. When they inevitably faced challenges—ups and downs in their respective careers, medical issues, long periods of separation when they were filming movies, and family members' health problems—that glue helped them persevere. "If it's that difficult to get together, you must really want to do it," says Michael.

The Arena Stage show they were in, *Moonchildren*, transferred to Broadway in 1972, so Jill and Michael moved to New York (taking their D.C. babysitter along with their meager collection of furniture). The show opened to rave reviews. But a week later, it closed.

"We were flat broke with a one-year-old in an apartment in the Village that we couldn't afford," says Michael. Thanks to unemployment insurance, they had $5 per week for food. "We ate a lot of spaghetti."

"In the pictures of us then, we are *really* thin," laughs Jill.

"Someone asked me the other day if it was a difficult time," continues Michael. "But it wasn't. It was a great time. We had nothing, but we were in New York."

They married in 1973, the day after Michael's divorce was final, in order to cement their custody of Alison. They had the ceremony performed in their apartment and invited a hot dog man up to cater the wedding. "That was it. Bring your own booze and have a hot dog," says Michael.

Thankfully, Jill's career started to take off, with roles on stage, then television, and eventually film. Meanwhile, Michael was floundering professionally.

"It was very frustrating," he says. "So I got out of [show] business. I started writing for a company that did sales meetings and trade shows. That supported us."

A challenge for any couple that works in the same field is a bit of professional competitiveness. There was some tension as their careers teeter-tottered.

"Her movement defined my stasis," says Michael. "And that was hard."

"But that's when you got into writing and writing has turned out to be the thing that you most love," says Jill. Michael nods. He has written three nonfiction books and recently published his first novel, *After Annie*.

When Jill began getting parts in film, including *Hide in Plain Sight* and *Arthur*, Michael was able to quit his copy-writing job and pursue acting again. After landing a role in Shakespeare in the Park, his stage career began to take off.

"Then my career took a dip. I had a really tough period where I wasn't getting roles I wanted," says Jill. "So I decided to get pregnant. We had our son, Max."

"That's when we realized that was going to be our life: one up and one down," says Michael. "And it was until this remarkable thing happened to us, which was *L.A. Law*."

The show's creator, Stephen Bochco, had been a classmate of Michael's at Carnegie Mellon. He asked the two of them to play an out-of-town couple on a two-part episode of *Hill Street Blues*.

"We had never really acted together before. We had been in the same plays, but she was the ingénue and I was the comedian in another scene," says Michael. "A year later, we found out it had been an audition to see if our chemistry translated on screen. And it did. So Stephen wrote the *L.A. Law* roles for us."

"We were pretty lucky," says Jill.

But the luck was mixed. Shortly after they shot the pilot for *L.A. Law*, Jill discovered a lump in her breast. "The first response was, 'This is it.' I'm going to die," says Jill. "People weren't telling success stories at that point."

But after Jill's lumpectomy at Mount Sinai in New York, they flew to L.A. to start shooting the series. Bochco helped arrange radiation treatments for her at UCLA each day after shooting. Now they describe the experience as a good thing. "When *L.A. Law* went on the air, it was a huge hit. We became famous. We were in magazines," says Jill. "But the breast cancer was a good way to keep our feet on the ground."

After *L.A. Law*'s eight-year run, Jill and Michael moved their family to Marin County in Northern California in 1995.

"We focused on our relationship," says Jill. "We had grabbed the brass ring, got the fame we wanted, all while looking mortality in the face. What seemed to be next was deepening our relationship instead of having it be far down on our priority list."

"We took some interesting courses," says Michael.

They took courses on tantra, communication, sex, and exploration of inner truths. "That opened our eyes to other possibilities in terms of how we could relate to each other," says Jill. "It was all about how to do it better, how to have more fun."

Twenty years into their marriage, it helped them reconnect.

"It was amazing to do this at that point in our lives," says Jill. "Because you can get comfortable. You take the whole thing for granted."

"In one course, we essentially told each other secrets we thought we would take to the grave," says Michael. "It was really dangerous stuff. When we got through that, we were really clean with each other. A whole cut deeper."

That kind of honesty can lead down some cobwebbed corridors and expose dark and disturbing things. "Yes, we're into that," says Jill, laughing.

They learned what the other really wanted, and how to make each other happy. And they learned to confront their deficits. Their mentor got Michael to see the depth of his male chauvinism and forced Jill to admit the degree to which she was in collusion with it. Recognizing these truths still allows them to deal with their conflicts more healthily.

"One of the most important things is to allow for change—in yourself and in the other," she continues. "In the other, it can be really scary. But in communication, anything is possible. And what we're learning is that there are many levels of communication. Our new word is *transparency*, just being completely transparent with each other."

The two even share a therapist, whom they visit separately. "We're on the fast track because she knows us both so well," says Jill. "As we get deeper and deeper into the sources of our individual issues, it expands our relationship like crazy."

It's also helped them work through bringing Jill's mother to live across the hall from them in their Upper West Side building. Jill's mother has dementia and needs full-time care. "Seeing my mother every day is like being in a therapeutic petri dish," says Jill. "It seemed like a calamity at first bringing her to the East Coast, but it's been fantastic."

This seems to be Jill and Michael's response to every difficulty. Dramatic challenges in their lives are opportunities to deepen and explore the contours of their relationship. When Jill had a recurrence of cancer in 2009, Michael worked through it by writing. His new novel is about a man whose wife dies of breast cancer.

"The glue thing—the understanding that we were meant to be together—is a huge part of being able to weather all this," says Jill. "Every adversity is an opportunity to see more clearly what the truth is about me and about us." ❉

About Cider Mill Press Book Publishers

Good ideas ripen with time. From seed to harvest, Cider Mill Press brings fine reading, information, and entertainment together between the covers of its creatively crafted books. Our Cider Mill bears fruit twice a year, publishing a new crop of titles each spring and fall.

Visit us on the Web at
www.cidermillpress.com
or write to us at
12 Port Farm Road
Kennebunkport, Maine 04046